it's called a spade

a collection of hard-to-tell true stories

JJ Barrows

WestBow Press books may be ordered through booksellers or by contacting:

WestBow Press
A Division of Thomas Nelson & Zondervan
1663 Liberty Drive
Bloomington, IN 47403
www.westbowpress.com
1 (866) 928-1240

Interior Image Credit: Jena Willard (author photo)

ISBN: 978-1-9736-7487-0 (sc)
ISBN: 978-1-9736-7488-7 (hc)
ISBN: 978-1-9736-7489-4 (e)

Library of Congress Control Number: 2019914070

Print information available on the last page.

WestBow Press rev. date: 9/23/2019

There are so many good women in this life.
This book is dedicated to at least three of them.

Lydia Jane Barrows
Thank you for giving me the push I needed to show up for life;
as long as I'm living, your baby I'll be.

Anna Elizabeth Stewart
"We're all real good and sad. Jesus will help us."
Let's hope so.

Emily Caroline Dauber
"Just call a spade a spade."
Okay, here I go ...

Contents

Introduction

My name is JJ, which is funny if you know the family I come from, a family of all B names (except my mother, Lydia, but she apparently has always liked the letter B because she married one and had three more).

My siblings are Bonnie, Bobby and Betsy. My dad is Bob. His siblings are Bonnie, Betty Ruth, Buddy, and Bill. My grandmother is Billie. My other grandparents are Ben and Betty. Our dogs are Buddy and Biscuit. Together we are the Barrows ... and I'm J.J.

I'm also a middle child. I remember the exact moment I realized my parents didn't run out of B names in the naming process. I was eating Cheerios. Just before finishing my multigrain goodness, it dawned on me. *Wait a second. I'm in the middle.* I had a complex about being skipped over for a really long time. Some people call it "middle-child syndrome," and maybe that's true, but having two Js in a B world didn't exactly help the syndrome. I no longer have a complex about being skipped over with the whole B thing, but I don't eat Cheerios anymore.

I am currently in my thirties, which is an awkward transitional age. The thirties are like adult puberty, where you're supposed to have everything figured out, but you don't and you can't say that. I was born with funny in my bones and just enough of a disconnect to be sad for no reason. Depending on the day and how much coffee I've had, I can have anywhere from above average to lowish self-esteem.

I was raised in the church, and I have spent time both loving and rejecting it due to my own issues and the need to be different.

Church or no church, I think most people can relate to having issues (or a particular set of skills) and wanting something greater than themselves while not being so certain about the options.

On top of uncertain options, you eventually grow up and realize your family isn't perfect; nor is anyone else. And yet with everyone trying so hard to be perfect but not talking about how hard life is, you begin to feel a little crazy and a little more like maybe there is no God after all.

For the record, I do think there is a God, but I'm not here to convince you of that. My thoughts and views of God have changed over the years of coming in and out of faith. Perhaps that's what I mean when I say this is a collection of "hard-to-tell" true stories; it's hard to admit when your faith is wavering, when the solid ground you've stood on for so long begins sinking, when you aren't sure whether you even want to believe in anything anymore.

Once I was sugarcoating a story to a friend without really being aware that that's what I was doing (sugarcoating is what southerners do to food; it makes anything taste good). Catching on to the fact that I was trying to present myself better than I seemed, felt, or believed, she stopped me and said, "I'm sorry, JJ. Can you just call a spade a spade?" I asked her what she meant, and she explained that in poker, people hold a straight face so as not to give away what cards they have. "It's how they bluff through the game. Your straight face is your smile. I see you smiling, appearing to be okay, and honey, you're beautiful, but I'm not so sure you're okay."

She was probably the first person to ever call me out, to see past my smile and take the time not only to ask but also to listen to what was really going on under the facade of unshakeable faith. Of course, unclogging years of stuff that was stuffed doesn't make for a quick and easy process. Just ask a plumber.

Call me a Late Learner, a Doubting Thomas, or a Debbie Downer, but I didn't know life could be hard and God could be good at the same time. I thought these thoughts were mutually exclusive, and you certainly couldn't voice otherwise.

For the sake of navigating through this book, I'll also refer to God as He or Him. This isn't a political or religious statement, or even a naive assumption, it's just the way I have come to personally communicate with the God I believe in. Nothing more, nothing less. Please don't read into it, life is hard enough without everyone picking each other apart for their differences. Sometimes when I see God's glory in that of a sunrise or a sunset, I tear up and whisper "Get it, Gurl!" And He gets it.

This is a collection of stories about life—about people and God, recovery and relapse, heartache and brokenness, and the reality that life is hard, even if you believe in God or you don't. But I also think there is hope and healing and that sometimes they come without answers. This is a collection of stories from a human who almost disappeared in her efforts to be seen, a girl who called spades hearts and smiled while bluffing.

Some stories are sad and deep; others are fun and lighthearted. Either way, it's just me simply trying to call it like I see it. Sometimes I'm sad, sometimes I'm funny, and sometimes I'm a little of both or neither ... and that, I'm still learning, is okay.

Part 1

It was an accident. I didn't wake up one morning and decide to relapse. I woke up one afternoon in the hospital and wondered how I had gotten there *again*. I was picked up off the cold, wooden floors of my living room in Portland, Oregon, carried to the car, and driven to the hospital for severe dehydration. It was May 5, 2013.

Six years after recovering from an eating disorder, I relapsed.

Nothing is ever as simple as it seems. I find it interesting when nonaddicts give addicts advice, such as, "Just stop drinking," "Just don't work as much," "Just eat," "Don't you know that throwing up your food is bad for you?", and "What about your electrolytes?" I'm pretty sure if things were that simple and we all cared about our electrolytes, no one would have any problems. We would all get along, and everyone would finally get what Miss America has been asking for this whole time: world peace.

But it's not that simple, and who cares about electrolytes when your heart is broken, your best friend dies, or your parents divorce? Advice to take care of yourself when everything is falling apart seems like the last thing you want someone to offer you, in part because not only is it not that simple but also it's the last thing you want to do. Take care of yourself. Hurting hurts, which is why most of us try to avoid it. We drink, we drug, we work, we run, we eat or don't eat. We do whatever it takes not to feel the hurt. Sometimes intentionally and sometimes not. Sometimes our addictions just happen because our default is to go for comfort over pain. Understandable.

I was ignorant of the small choices I had made over time. I didn't realize they were going to add up to a hospital bed *again*. In the moment, they seemed really small—insignificant even. In retrospect, math was right: even the smallest of things add up to a really big thing.

I think it might have been Jack Sparrow who said, "The problem isn't the problem. The problem is your problem with the problem." I had a problem: how I dealt with life's problems.

This is life. It's good, it's hard, and it happens in ways we least expect. Problems surface every day all the time, so the question isn't, How can we stop problems from happening? The question is, How do we respond to problems when they happen? When what you feel hurts and you don't want to feel it, taking care of yourself sounds like less of a good idea and more like facing a reality you don't want to be your reality.

It took waking up in a hospital bed to realize things had been hard for a while and that I apparently wasn't handling them very well. In the summer of 2013, I set about for recovery again. But not only were there problems I needed to deal with; there was also the problem of where I was in life while trying to recover.

I was still coming to terms with accepting my pastoral parents' divorce after thirty years of marriage, having my heart broken multiple times by the same person, and honestly not knowing what to do with my life after thirty years of living it. The only thing I seemed to be good at was messing up except for one thing: being the lunch lady.

I was a full-time cook at a preschool in southeast Portland.

When I first took on the job, I thought I was getting better, because I was at my job. But the more I obsessed over the food I made at work, the easier it became to hide my own obsession outside work. And the more obsessed I was with something, the less hard all the other stuff seemed. It seemed only natural to keep obsessing if it made the pain go away. But the pain wasn't decreasing. My distraction from the pain was increasing.

Being the lunch lady was the first job I felt good at; it paid well, and that was finally making other people proud. "JJ grew up and got a real job," people said. Or at least a salaried job, which was a big deal to anyone who knew the transient in me. The better I got at my job, the more I impressed people; and the more I impressed people, the more I thought I needed my job to make me okay. Perhaps that was part of the problem. I was trying to make me okay without admitting I wasn't okay.

When 2013 wrapped up, I found myself in the hospital again. By that time, December, I knew something had to change. But change takes time, and I wasn't ready yet. As a creature of habit, I was set in my problematic ways.

Early in 2014, I knew it was time to let go of being the lunch lady. I talked to God about this decision a lot. I didn't hear a whole lot back (at least I don't think I did; I'm still not sure how it all works), but I felt like it was okay for me to want to be okay.

Find Your Pace

It's funny how life works, how you can wake up with vigor in the morning, ready to take on the day, only to be sad by lunch and wonder why any of it matters. Or vice versa. I haven't yet decided which order of emotions a day can bring that I most prefer. I suppose I'd rather finish strong than start well, at least with most things in life, but waking up sad is no motivation to get out of bed either.

Today I woke up with vigor, ready to take on the day and show it who was boss. I'm not quite sure whether it had to do with writing again after a long hiatus, reactivating my Facebook account, or discovering I could play Scrabble on my phone, but I must admit to being excited over these little things in life. Not to mention I lived on a pond where I woke up every morning to the sound of birds in the trees and ducks landing on the water. No big deal, except it was.

It is certainly not every day that I wake up with such vigor, but I warmly welcome the days when I do, knowing the vigor may fade and my mood may change. But also it may not. I am learning to allow room for the day to hold great possibilities along with great impossibilities. I may not be capable of doing the impossible, but as of right now, I'm on speaking terms with God, and rumor has it God makes all things possible. I'm still not quite sure how that all works or how I get in on that, but I think it at least means there is always hope.

That's a good start.

Anybody can start something, such as a day, a job, a race, a book, a good intention, or a "till death do us part," but it takes a lot of hard work to actually finish something with the same vital force you started it with, especially if you want to finish it well.

I'll be honest: I am excellent at starting things, which is the reason I have more rough drafts than I do publications. Aside from a blog, I have never published anything (spoiler alert: that changes). I have nothing on paper. I have no words you can hold in your hands, hear as you turn the pages, and smell as you open a new book (ahem). While I have made attempts to publish a thing or two outside of a virtual reality, most of those attempts consisted of Word documents started at five o'clock in the morning, interrupted by breakfast followed by work and a nap, and I never looked at them again until years later. After I had a breakdown, I went back to search my documents in need of a reminder that while I might feel stunted or like I should be further along, I have come an incredibly long way.

Finishing something is a much harder task for me. I'm easily distracted. I like shiny objects. I get hungry. There are numerous reasons why I don't finish things, some of which are legitimate human reasons, such as eating, and some of which are not, like Pinterest, Instagram, and the black hole that is Google.

The other week, I started a load of laundry. I did a great job of loading the machine, putting the detergent in the right spot, and hitting the start button. Oh, how I love to start something! Truly, it was a beautiful act of cleanliness that was a long time coming. But then I forgot all about the start button, and that there is almost always a whole other part to the process of finishing the laundry. I forgot until three days later when I wasn't even going to check the laundry but to look for a painting I had found imperative to find the moment I sat down to write. On my way to the basement, where I have a few of my paintings stored, I passed the washing machine, which I am better acquainted with than the neglected dryer sitting next to it.

To make a long story short, I had to wash my clothes again since they had sat for too long in a damp state. And guess what didn't happen as I refilled the washing machine and restarted my load before leaving the basement? Locating the painting I had gone to the basement to find in the first place.

I'm easily distracted. I like shiny objects. I get hungry.

Last year, I started my job as a preschool cook with such quickness and dexterity that I thought I was going to unite tots from all over the world and start a food revolution. I imagined posters with their little fists in the air and spaghetti sauce on their little mouths. I don't even like spaghetti sauce. I somehow manage to dream big while not dreaming big at all. I don't want to start a food revolution; I don't even know what that means. I want to write and not even about food, but get me started on something, and I will go at it with such great force that I might land myself in a hospital due to brake failure. Sometimes I don't finish things simply because I don't want to, and sometimes I don't finish things simply because I can't, because I have made it physically impossible to move forward.

"Find your pace!" a sticky note on my desk says, a reminder that should have been there long before the two hospital bands I now keep as souvenirs that found themselves on my wrists last year.

Start strong, find your pace, and finish well.

In regard to my job, I started strong. I don't mean to toot my own horn, but I do because I did; I started strong. And I don't even say that to brag necessarily; if anything it's embarrassing to say I'm just over a year into a job and I've already peaked. Will words like *endurance, perseverance,* and *longevity* ever be part of my vernacular or, more importantly, the way I live my life? I say I started strong as part of my confession that the strength I started with was mostly my own; the horse I rode in on I had picked out myself. And while I thanked God for the wonderful opportunity, I kindly told Him to step aside. "I'll take it from here," I said in response to a gift that was meant to work more like a Groupon to be shared than a coupon to be cashed in for a better deal on something I wanted. I can't imagine what "I'll take it from here" must sound like in the ears of God; what's worse, I can't imagine how often He hears it, and what's worse still, how often He hears it from me.

There are many ways I could wrap up what I am trying to say, or I could just stay true to form and leave it unfinished, introducing it to a multitude of other rough drafts from my past. But I refuse to let what *has been* true to form for me in the past be true to form for me *now.* I have been set free in more ways than one from who I used to be, and so even though it has taken me a while, and even though I may still do things like forget the laundry or get lost on Pinterest, I will live in the freedom of who I am now.

Old habits die hard, but I'm not who I used to be. I may have to restart the laundry a few times before mastering the whole process, but I take pride in the fact that my pins on Pinterest are starting to look more like inspirational quotes than recipes for how to avoid butter. And for the record, I like butter. I will be honest and say that in some ways, for whatever reason, I am afraid of butter, so that's me being honest, but me being brave is saying I actually like butter, and I won't let my fear of it keep me from eating out with friends. I'm more like myself than I ever have been, mostly because I'm more unlike who I was before.

Part of finding my pace in life and trying to live it well is looking at the places where maybe I don't need to keep up the pace at all, places where I need to stop. This isn't quitting or another excuse to leave something unfinished; it is prioritizing and accepting the fact that I can't do everything, which is probably the exact reason why so many things get left undone. I try to do it all, spreading myself thin, wearing myself out, and leaving promises unkept and projects unfinished. When a mere mortal takes on an "I can do everything for everyone all the time" mentality and tries to approach life in that way, a lot of things are going to get left undone, a lot of people are going to be left disappointed, and a lot of laundry will end up smelling more like a wet car seat than fresh lavender. Let's face it, folks. We can't do it all for everyone all the time ... *and that's okay.*

My job as the lunch lady is coming to an end this month, and a new journey is beginning. I am a mix of nerves and excitement, peace and chaos, confusion and clarity, dust and divine breath. Unlike many other things I have given up on, I don't consider this to be giving up. I consider it to be moving forward, perhaps not in the way the world sees it. Despite the fact that in many ways I used my job as a means to hide and not deal with life, a lot of good has come from it, and I don't regret for one second having done it. My job as the lunch lady has played a huge part in shaping me into the me I am right now.

And the me I am right now? Well, if we're calling a spade a spade, the me I am right now is someone who is learning how to live as she recovers from an eating disorder, again. Humbling. I always prided myself on telling people I was in recovery from an eating disorder. I never thought I would have to say "again." Ever. Once was enough, thank you. Yet here I sit, looking back on the last year when I barely survived, and I must accept the fact that for as much as I don't want to be "that girl," my struggle is my struggle. If I don't start by owning it, I will never overcome it. For me to work as a cook while trying to recover from an eating disorder is about as helpful as a recovering alcoholic trying to work at a bar. I just can't do it.

Perhaps there was more I could have done or not done to have avoided relapse, I don't know. That's the trouble with a relapse; it's not usually a snap decision. It's a mere baby step, a seemingly insignificant inch that in and of itself probably isn't that big of a deal. But it's baby step after baby step after baby step that has you heading down a path where you don't want to go, and it lands you in a place where you don't want to be, wondering how in the name of Sam, whoever he is, you ended up there in the first place.

I still have three weeks left at my job, and my goal is to finish well, to be fully present, and to be all in while I am there, accepting the fact that it's okay to say, "I can't do this anymore." I may be stepping down from a position that gave me a lot of purpose in life as well as the ability to pay my rent, but I feel as though I'm stepping up in life, owning my story, and fully living in it instead of running away from it.

And so here I am, at thirty years old, beginning to learn how to live my life well, again. I'm finding my pace and trying not to forget to switch over the laundry in the process, if for no other reason than the sweet smell of even the smallest victories.

All Day Long

I put Parker to bed after we sprayed his red pillowcase with water from a spray bottle wrapped in tinfoil. Parker is my favorite kid to babysit. "It keeps the nightmares away," he whispered, and he asked me to lie down next to him. Parker has a twin bed with a guard rail, so I lay on the floor and rested my hand on his bed to assure him I was there. He stretched out his little hand and put it on top of mine.

He traced the top of my hand with his fingers before settling them in between mine and holding my hand, giving it a few squeezes. His fingers retreated from holding to go back to tracing, settling back in, holding, squeezing, retreating, tracing. It was sort of like an artist feeling the tension of wanting to engage in his art but also holding the hand of the person he loves. I'm not saying Parker loves me. I know the girls in his class he has crushes on, but I know he loved my being there in that moment in the darkness of his room just before he nodded off to sleep.

I lay on the floor by his bed, and together we listened to instrumental lullabies streaming from his mom's iPod, which was plugged into the speakers in his room. I was in no rush to leave him, but the piano was starting to lull me to sleep, and I didn't want his parents to get home and find the babysitter passed out on the floor, so

I told him I would stay for a few more minutes before going downstairs and promising to come back and check on him. Just as I was about to get up, I froze and stopped dead in my tracks because of the next song playing gently in the background on the iPod piano.

It was a song my dad used to hum to my siblings and me before bed. We made up our own words, taking turns singing and humming the beautiful melody. We sang things like "I love flowers, I love sunshine, I love music, I love puppies ... all day long." The song was different every time we sang it because we always changed up who or what we loved, sometimes loving Oreos and peanut butter, other times loving Mommy and Daddy. But no matter who or what we loved, the song always ended with "all day long."

I had no idea until tonight while lying there on Parker's floor that my dad hadn't made up that melody. This is the tune of my childhood, and though it's not at the forefront of my mind every day, I have never forgotten it. This tune is as vivid a memory as my first visit from the tooth fairy or pushing Daniel Eggert off the playground in sixth grade. And I had no idea it was an actual song, an actual lullaby a lot of kids actually go to sleep to. I'd never heard that song outside my dad's humming and singing about the things he loved all day long, but there it was, on Parker's mom's iPod, some three thousand miles away from the place I had first heard it and the man I thought had created it.

Parker was still holding on to my hand, and I rolled over just enough so my face was buried into the floor while lying on my side. He squeezed my hand as I rolled over, and with my dad's lullaby playing in the background, as quietly as I could, I cried. I'm crying now as I try to write this while back at home, still listening to the song, because I found it on iTunes and purchased five different renditions of it. I'm kind of a masochist who can't really finish crying just because she finished babysitting.

The song is titled "All the World Is Sleeping," but the only thing I can hear when I hear it is a list of things I love "all day long."

"All day long" was the most important part of the song because it solidified the fact that you loved that thing, the fact that you loved it all day long and not just sometimes. And I think love *should* be like that, all day long, at least with people. Taste buds change, and hairstyles do too, and we should all be glad we don't love eighties hair anymore, but people aren't as easy to rid yourself of as bad hair, or at least they shouldn't be.

"All day long" means even on an off day, even when you are cranky, hungry, angry, hangry, sad, bloated, hormonal, forgetful, careless, depressed, apathetic, I might not feel like loving you, but I choose to love you ... all day long. Your emotions cannot scare me away any more than mine can tell me how to love you; I choose you, good and bad, forgetful and depressed, and angry and bloated. I love you ... all day long.

And while it was nostalgic to hear that song and be taken straight back to my childhood, as if a time machine had warped me there, it was also heartbreaking. It was heartbreaking not because I found out at thirty that my dad hadn't actually made up my bedtime song; it was heartbreaking because "all day long" no longer applies to my family, at least not to my parents. And I don't know how ready I am to talk on the matter, the matter of divorce, but it is certainly a matter to be talked about, at least at some point.

It's a matter to be talked about because it is real, and pretending it's not isn't going to bring back the naivety of my childhood, which allowed me to think everything was fine between Mommy and Daddy. And it is a matter to be talked about not because I want to throw anybody under the bus or rip the carpet out from under anyone but because it is a matter to be talked about because I'm tired of the lumpy carpet, hiding everything that gets swept under it, and standing on top of it with a pretty smile. No one likes a lumpy carpet.

I get that there are safe people and places and all sorts of books on boundaries for addressing such an issue, and I will do my best to respect what and who I can in this process. I have no desire to air dirty laundry for the sake of making others smell what I smell, especially seeing as how the stench won't lessen in my own nostrils simply because it reaches the fringe of someone else's. But I will also say that I won't silently live in fear anymore of what other people think of me, if they think anything at all (I think I give too much power to that thought).

And I will not silently live in fear anymore of what other people think of my pastor father and mother, now divorced after thirty some years, even if not to silently live in fear anymore simply means to directly say aloud, "I am sad over something worth being sad about."

I love my parents, both of them. I love them all day long, even on the sad days. And I know God loves them right where they are, even if right where they are is hurting not only them but also me. I love them, and I'm sad, and I love them. It's not one or the other; it's both/and. This may be obvious to some, but for those raised in a southern church environment, divorce is a touchy subject, almost as much as homosexuality or voting Democrat.

I have a certain experience with the church, and then I have a certain experience with Jesus, the guy the church talks about; and I hate to say it, but the two are pretty different.

I believe Jesus loves divorced people just as much as He loves married people, gay people as much as straight people, suburbanite people as much as city people, and people with homes as much as people without them. This list of seemingly opposite people, who really aren't all that opposite when the social, political, and religious barriers are removed, goes on and on, and I believe Jesus loves them all because the descriptive isn't what Jesus is all about. Jesus is all about the person.

Jesus is all about the person. Jesus *loves* people, and His life is reflective of that. Mine? Not so much except for a few people I'm really good at loving. I think I have a hard time loving people, because loving people has a lot to do with sharing, be it time, money, food, or whatever the other is in need of. And while I might be good at giving, I've never been good at sharing, which is evident by the fact that my first word was "mine." I will give you something I don't want or need or that I can afford to let go of, because that's not a sacrifice. But share my cinnamon roll? Are you kidding me? Gluten free is expensive. Go get your own cinnamon roll.

I want to love people, but most of the time, I don't want to do what it takes to love them, at least not all day long. I want to *say* I love people without having to act on it. I want to know what the cinnamon roll tastes like so I can offer some sort of insight to those who are on the fence about the cinnamon roll. And I want to play a part, take some sort of credit for why they chose to get the cinnamon roll for breakfast instead of eggs, but I certainly don't want to have to share *my* cinnamon roll in the process. And as they delight in the ooey-gooey goodness of the warm cinnamon roll they have chosen, I want to say, "See, I told you!" without ever having to experience the discomfort of giving something up.

So there's my spade to reveal. I want the "See, I told you. I knew it" without the "Here you go. Have some of mine." I want the glory without the sacrifice. And that looks nothing like the Jesus I claim to know and love. And thus it proves once again that I could never be God because I can't even sacrifice a bite of a cinnamon roll, let alone a family member.

So there I lay on the floor in Parker's room, thinking of my family members and listening to a song I honestly thought I would never hear again except in a memory somewhere. My dad and we kids were the only ones who knew the tune to that song, or so I thought, and the days of us being tucked into bed have been long gone for some time now. And while all the world lay sleeping, or at least while Parker lay sleeping, I listened to the lost song from my childhood, and I grieved. I grieved the brokenness of my family. I grieved the brokenness of people because none of us are exempt from being hurt or from hurting people … not even the pastor, the pastor's wife, or the pastor's kids. We hurt each other, we hurt people, we hurt. Curled up in a ball on the floor in the dark, the big, strong babysitter held the hand of the four-year-old little boy who was afraid of nightmares, and she cried.

Tempted to go back downstairs and start watching Netflix, I thought about what Parker might need in that moment instead of what would make me most comfortable, which was certainly not his floor. And let's be honest. Who wants to cry over something that hurts when they could go watch *Thelma & Louise* instead? And while it wasn't a cinnamon roll that was being asked of me to share, since it was much too late and the sugar wouldn't have done Parker well before bed, it was the holding of my left hand and a little more of my time to just be near him, a proverbial cinnamon roll, so to speak, that he needed.

And so I stayed. I lay on the discomfort of Parker's floor and felt the discomfort of my parents' recent divorce, and I quietly cried as I held the hand of a little boy who was on the fence about sleeping alone.

"All day long," I sang over and over to no one in particular as I listed the things and people I loved, the secret words to this apparently well-known lullaby. Those three words remain stuck in my head, replaying over and over ... "all day long," even at the end of the day when all you want to do is check out and watch *Thelma & Louise* (not that it's not okay for there to be a time for that).

As I tuck myself in for the night, I say to myself and anyone willing to listen, "Don't miss out on where you might need to be loving someone, even if it makes you uncomfortable, even if you have to keep doing it 'all day long.'"

No matter how long the day is, life is much too short not to love someone for the length of it.

No Tents in Sight

This morning I woke up to the sound of math in my head. Let it be said that I hate math- more than black licorice, more than romantic comedies, and more than having to wear wet socks all day. I truly, truly hate math. I failed math twice in high school, landing myself in my younger brother and sister's math class, two grades below me. Not one grade below me but *two* grades below me. Given such a strong emotion for the subject matter, you can see how this was quite an unpleasant sound to wake up to, all of it occurring in the space between my ears in the wee hours of the morning. Doing numbers, calculating, adding, subtracting, multiplying ... hours by days, days by weeks, weeks by months, and months by wages—even more numbers with decimals. It was horrible.

I can conclude only that I woke up to the sound of math in my head because my job is coming to an end within the next three weeks, but my payment for living life is not. I can conclude this was the reason because I was multiplying what I need to make per hour by a certain number of days per week to pay to live in my house each month. When I realized the job I was debating to take on would only pay me in a month what I make now in a week, I panicked.

"That can't be right," I said to myself, knowing my math skills were well below average, so I pulled out a modern-day calculator, also known as a smartphone, and I checked my work as well as the time. Lo and behold, it was 4:46 a.m., and the calculator for once was on my side, telling me I was in fact correct. There was a brief moment of triumph for being as smart as my phone and being correct on an issue that involved numbers, followed by realizing I had forgotten to include monthly payments for my intelligent phone in all my equations and settling on the unnerving fact that I had no idea how I was going to do this … this life thing, or at least pay for it.

I feel confident moving in the direction I am going. I have peace about leaving my job, even with it being essential to my well-being. I rest assured that the Lord had spoken, and I said I would follow, even if I didn't know where we were going. Yes, my cup runneth over with the sweet peace of Jesus and the luscious smells of basil and watermelon as I waft through a field of poppies, careless in the care of God, pursuing my best life now.

And for a split second in the day, that is true, and I am almost tempted to buy the book … And then there is the rest of the day, which involves bills and laundry and broken things like scooters and glasses and contact lenses that go dry and shrivel up like an old lady. You desperately try to revive them with the cheapest form of contact solution you can find because even if you could afford more contacts, you certainly couldn't afford to keep them moisturized, and by "you" I mean me. But speaking of moisture, water is free to drink, depending on where you come from, but it's not free to use, so you bank on the money-saving phrase you learned as a child, "When it's yellow, let it mellow. When it's brown, flush it down," hoping that all that mellowing is going to buy you more time in the house you don't want to leave, even though it's swarmed with ants that *just won't die.* Then there are the dishes in the sink; no matter how many times you wash them, so long as you eat food, even if it's from a can because cans are cheap and dented cans are even cheaper (much like the little ants that have made their way into every part of the house), *the dishes just won't go away.*

And those are just my own first-world issues. I don't even know how or where to begin with all the weighted thoughts about how and what to do about the third world, about poverty and starvation and sex trafficking, not just on another continent but within the city limits of where I live. When living in this world, beautiful as it is—and hear me say that loud and clear, *beautiful as it is*—keep in mind that it's also dark and often chaotic, even as a follower of Jesus. Dare I say, especially as a follower of Jesus.

And you wake up calculating, configuring, and engaging in a subject that has told you since at least the seventh grade that you are well below average and will never amount to anything so long as numbers are involved; and while I prefer words over numbers anyway (and spending my days in the company of words is a nice enough thought), the fact of the matter is, for as much as I hate numbers and they hate me, I need to at least learn to be okay with numbers in some form, even if not in abundance, to simply partake in this thing called life.

There are a number of ways I could take this conversation (see that, numbers; I can't escape them, even in my words), and I don't know how much I want to jump into any of those ways before an eight-hour workday, which I get is average. But I've been up since 4:30 a.m., and so my pride wants a cookie of some sort or at least the click of a like button on social media. Spades are ugly, but I refuse to call them hearts.

And so all these anxiety-inducing numbers got me thinking. I used to think adulthood would be some sort of sanctuary, a citadel, a fortress, in which I would be safe from all I had been afraid of as a child; it was like these invisible walls of being an adult would protect me from my fears. Fears like Pete the Hag (a traumatizing ghost story told by my sixth-grade teacher) or the fact that Zack Vernon liked Katie Parker and Brian Justice liked Lauren what's-her-face with the blonde hair, who developed well before all the other girls did. No one liked me because I looked more like a little boy than a little girl, and *would I ever be picked first for anything?*

Or the fact that one day my parents would get old and unnoticeable, which as a kid seemed worse than dying. There's an honest and morbid thought that often freaked me out and stopped me dead in my tracks while swinging from a tree. I thought that all those fears, worries, and anxieties would no longer be an issue when I walked through the gates of adulthood, safe and protected from the helpless feeling of being a child on the run from a ghost story, permanently underdeveloped and anxious about the formality of old age.

Last year I turned thirty, and while Pete the Hag is no longer an issue, I believe there is an enemy on the prowl. I still have a lot of insecurity about the boy I like liking other girls and the fact that I'm still holding out hope for a growth spurt. Not only are my parents getting old but now I am too, and most of the people I encounter on an everyday basis think my first name is Miss as opposed to JJ. Adulthood was supposed to protect me. I was supposed to be fearless and unaffected by the fears of a child, and while I am grateful to be right where I am without a desire to go back or rush forward, there are days when I honestly think I just can't do this grown-up stuff. Why did I rush so much to get here?

I have yet to find such a sanctuary, such a citadel, such a fortress in this world that protects me from the fears, worries, and anxieties of this life. "A mighty fortress is our God." I know; I've heard my granddad sing it my whole life. "God himself is in her citadels." Yes, descendants of Korah, I agree with your psalms. "You should have eaten the goat in the sanctuary area, as I commanded." Wait, what was that, God? I'm still sorting through Leviticus. Honestly, I'm still sorting through most of the Bible. But even more honestly, I sometimes don't care enough to sort at all.

And I don't say, "I know, I know. God is the answer," as if to imply that's a nice enough idea but not really applicable to life, because I think scripture is more than just a nice enough idea and very applicable to life. I say that to say that while I agree with David, who said in Psalms that I can dwell in God's tent forever and take refuge in the shelter of

His wings, I also agree with Jesus, who said, "In this world *you will have trouble*" (John 16:33 NIV. Emphasis added).

And don't worry. I know He doesn't stop there. I know He follows that up with, "But take heart, for I have overcome the world." And I do; I take heart. But I guess that's just it; there have to be trials, sorrow, and trouble to even obey the command to take heart. If everything was fine and dandy, and smelled like basil and watermelon all the time, there would be no need to take heart. There would be no need for the world to be overcome. There would be no need for Jesus. Right? Maybe?

I don't know, but I need something or someone greater than me, and the kindest, most loving thing or man I've ever heard of or encountered up to this point in my life is Jesus. And at this point, I'll take it. Or Him… I'll take Him.

Tangibly speaking, there is no sanctuary, no citadel, no fortress to protect me from my own thoughts. I'm open to debate on that, but I can think the most horrible things inside a church as I can outside a church, so mere walls with stained-glass windows aren't going to protect me from negative thoughts or fears of the unknown. And I guess if I'm honest, I'm still trying to sort through what it looks like on this side of eternity for God to be my sanctuary. I find it just as hard to think of myself as hiding in the shelter of God's wings. My pastor, Josh, says he finds it hard to think of himself as the "bride" of Christ. Some men have a hard time being referred to as a bride. That makes sense to me, and I can't say I blame them (some men don't mind being referred to as a bride, and that's okay too). I have a hard time thinking of God as a father *and* of having wings. So it goes with our mortal minds being unable to grasp what is immortal.

I don't know whether it's just a translation thing, but I like when David says, "I will dwell in God's tent forever," because tents I understand, at least more so than tabernacles and sanctuaries. Citadels I have a mild concept of only because I went to college in South Carolina. The military college of the South, The Citadel, was stationed just a few miles down the road from my own liberal arts college. I even dated a few Citadel cadets, and while they looked cute in their uniforms behind all that heightened security, I didn't exactly walk away from that season of life with a great example of a mighty stronghold, excited about the notion that God was my citadel. If anything, I hoped God didn't drink as much as they did, but that is neither here nor there; and we all have our stuff. I was no peach in college.

My point was tents. Tents I understand because tents I have both built and found myself in for as long as I can remember. My siblings and I would build these massive multi-room tents or forts in our living room out of the kitchen chairs and sheets straight off the bed. They were fully equipped with white Christmas lights and kitchen appliances for fake baking. Sometimes we had the luxury of leaving our tents up for the whole weekend, playing "camp out," "olden days," or "Queen of Sheba." Being that we were kids without cable, fort building was essential to our upbringing, be it inside or out. Most of the good and safe memories of my childhood involve a tent of some kind.

I understand a tent as a safe place because that is exactly what it was when I was a child. Whether in the living room or out in the wilderness, even if I heard something grumbling on the other side (a wild animal or my dog, Biscuit), for some reason it felt like that thin sheet of fabric made me invisible to any potential harm or the need to grow up too quickly. I felt safe from the fears of my childhood and from feeling like I had to be anybody other than me.

I am an intense person. I think way too much, and I feel a depth of emotion that shouldn't be physically possible, so I know I'm not the easiest person to do life with, which sometimes makes me nervous to be me. I think perhaps that is why I like tents so much, because I'm intense, and in tents I am me.

I still feel that way sometimes as I crawl under my comforter and make a tent for one. I don't know why feeling invisible feels safe, but it does. If I'm not seen, I can't be harmed, so all too often, I hide. And this morning I wasn't hiding per se, but I was safely under my tent (my bedspread), waiting to wake up to either the sound of an alarm or the push of Mother Nature, but something very unsafe and unwanted crept in instead. Numbers. Numbers asked me what I thought I was doing, who I thought I was, and how I thought I was going to get away with this—with being me, with pursuing life outside an eating disorder, outside a relationship, outside a well-paying job. As I weighed the odds, they were not in my favor, and then I told those odds to get out of my tent.

The truth is, I don't know how I am going to do this. I don't have answers. Adulthood spared me no fear, and though God did and does dwell in the tents of my stories, He also dwells outside them. While my God may be referred to as a safe place, a place of refuge, a citadel, so to speak, He is not limited to them, only to be found in places that are safe. He is not a place or a structure, a genie, or a fortune cookie. While He is consistent in who He is, He has never followed a formula with me or taught me the same lesson without a new insight. He has never replicated a sunset, tossed the same wave, or orchestrated the same thunderstorm. He is the same, and He is not the same all at the same time; and for as much as it makes sense, it doesn't. He doesn't make sense to me in my best efforts to understand Him; He doesn't make sense to me.

Anybody who can claim to know the number of grains of sand on the beaches' vastitude or the number of hairs on each head across the span of history could never, ever make sense to me. He's a numbers guy while at the same time He's not at all because He cares about *this one*, and *that one*, and each *one person*; regardless of how much hair is on his or her or their head, He cares about him, her or their. I can't keep up, but God can.

As a thirty-year-old, I still have fears. In this adult world I still have trouble. I would have no need to take heart if I didn't have trouble, and taking heart is one of my favorite things to do because to me it's one of the most beautiful things I think Jesus said, in part because it acknowledges the ugly while welcoming the beautiful. Taking heart doesn't mean pretending there is no trouble. Taking heart means having hope and being bold in the midst of trouble. Everybody wants to say they are taking heart, but nobody wants to say they are having trouble. You need to address the trouble before you can flaunt the fact that you are taking heart. In my opinion, don't say you need Jesus unless you are willing to say why, even if it's as simple and vague as saying "because I'm a mess."

And so I'm a mess. There is trouble in my life, and I suppose it's all relative, but that doesn't make it any less trouble for me. And though there is trouble, I'm taking heart because my hope is in Someone greater than all the forts, sanctuaries, and tents built over the span of time. And while I may not know what I am doing next (and that terrifies me), I am taking heart because my hope is in Someone greater than my fears and in Someone who cares. He cares about the little things, the little people, and the little thoughts that creep in and try to tell us otherwise.

I'm taking heart by being active in my hope that leaving my job is the next best step for me. I am being active by doing things I don't even really want to do but know I need to do. I am updating my résumé, job hunting, and doing my part to figure out what's next, trusting Him with any doors that may be involved. While I love to hide in my tents, even as an adult, I am being bold by not sitting around on my bed "just taking heart and trusting Jesus to give me a job." I am taking heart *and* trusting Him while doing something with those two facts at hand.

Many hours have passed since I started writing this morning, and while this might not have anything to do with anything, this afternoon I laid out in the sun on my deck and talked to God. "I love the sun, I love the water, I love the sound of the birds … and my heart is broken." Perhaps the broken-heart bit is a story for another day, but it struck me as it came out of my mouth that while what I loved didn't minimize my broken heart, my broken heart didn't minimize what I loved.

I named what I loved, and instead of saying, "*But* my heart is broken," as if none of what I loved mattered, I named what I loved and said, "*And* my heart is broken," allowing there to be room for both love and heartache. And even if it was just for that brief moment this afternoon, holding the weight of love and heartache together, I felt like I knew Jesus really well, and taking heart seemed more possible than ever.

And it all happened out in the open with no tents in sight.

Rosemary High Fives

Last week I wrote about my parents' divorce on my blog. I know ... divorce again? But bear with me. I think I'm almost done processing. And even if I'm not done hurting, feeling, or trying to make sense of it all, I firmly believe in the light at the end of the tunnel, and the occasional matchstick along the way, even if I fumble in the dark for a bit.

It still sounds weird for the concept of my parents' divorce to exit my mind and see the words fully exposed, lingering in the air as it reaches a friend's ear or there on a page in front of me. I don't know which is weirder, speaking it out or writing it out. Both are weird in their own ways, and *weird* isn't even an adequate word. But then again, what word is adequate when talking about divorce? *Weird* seems appropriate enough because there's nothing normal about divorce. And I don't even know what "normal" is or looks like anymore, especially since I've been living in Portland for the last three years, and the town's slogan is literally "Keep Portland Weird." People live up to that slogan by donning top hats as they ride double-decker bicycles, Hula-Hoop on their way to a floating session, or dance with nunchucks that have been soaked in kerosene and set ablaze every last Thursday of the month. You can see how my definition of *normal* has been slightly skewed over the years. I no longer do a double-take when walking past a clown sitting on a park bench. I have been desensitized, you might say. Weird is now normal.

Weird is now normal, which is what is funny to me about the whole "Keep Portland Weird" thing. People are going to exhaust themselves trying *not* to be normal, because they have in effect made weird normal, and they can't live up to their own slogan of keeping it weird if they aren't, in fact, weird.

So I don't know what weird looks like, but I know what it feels like. I might look "normal" to the Hula-Hoopers and fire dancers, but I don't *feel* normal. I don't need avant-garde clothing or hobbies to express the fact that nothing about how I feel right now feels normal.

Nothing feels normal about being thirty because I've never been thirty before last year. Nothing feels normal about quitting a salaried job because I've never quit a salaried job before this year, nor have I even had a salaried job before last year. Nothing feels normal about eating a minimum of three times a day—six if you're including snacks—because while I maybe nailed the whole eating thing as a kid, it's been over a decade since I started failing at it.

Nothing feels normal about being a kid whose parents are divorced because I've never been a kid whose parents are divorced. I've only been a thirty-year-old whose parents are divorced, so I'm trying to figure not only out how one handles divorce but how one handles divorce as an adult. I wasn't spared any pain just because I was an adult with an understanding of the definition and reasons behind divorce when I was told, "Mommy and Daddy aren't going to live together anymore."

I don't feel like an adult, and I most certainly don't feel thirty, at least not the thirty they show in the movies. Just this morning, I was trying to reheat my coffee in a pot over a portable plug-in stove top because I don't have a microwave; nor do I have a stove, so I bought a plug-in stove top from Goodwill for $7.99. Coffee and bargain-shopping seem adult enough, and I almost gave myself credit for that, but as I started to congratulate myself for acting my age while warming up my morning adult beverage, I got distracted and spilled some of my coffee on the counter.

No big, I thought, and I reached for a paper towel, only to realize I didn't have any paper towels. So I reached for a dish towel, only to realize I didn't have any dish towels. So I reached for a hand towel, only to realize I didn't have any of those either. I looked around my one room of a house (in other words, a studio) as I stood in the corner deemed the kitchen and debated using a sock from the corner deemed the laundry room, but something seemingly adult-ish in me told me that using a dirty sock to wipe up the counter might be gross. As I looked around the room, canceling out blankets and beanies as possible candidates to wipe up my slight mess, I looked down at my sweatpants. Before I could even reach the "Aha!" part of my thought, I was lifting my knee to the height of the counter and wiping up the spilled coffee with the sweatpants *I was wearing*.

Just as I was thinking that I should probably do some kid-friendly adult things today like invest in paper towels, I lost my balance. It's been a while since I've done yoga, and the whole tree pose was never in my favor anyway. I'm more of a downward-dog type person, so I'm not sure what I was thinking while actually taking the time to think while standing on one leg and simultaneously wiping down my counter with the clothes I was wearing; but there I was, thinking, wiping, and dirtying my clothes all in one act, all on one leg. And I almost believed I was the grand master of multitasking, until I lost my balance.

As I started to go down, the knee I was wiping the counter with ended up kneeing the pot my coffee was in, knocking the entire pot over and turning the original tiny spill into Lake Placid there on my countertop. I managed to catch myself before landing on the floor but only at the expense of reaching for the nearest thing in sight to grab for support, which was a rack of clean dishes. Said dishes were no longer clean, and a few of them suffered the same fate as Humpty Dumpty. All the king's horses and all David's mighty men couldn't put my dishes back together again.

While I stood there, looking at the larger mess I had made, I noticed my jar of honey on the counter, soaking in a pool of coffee. I snatched the jar up quickly to wipe it off, as if the coffee was going to ruin the jar, only to remember seconds after my snatching that I didn't have anything to wipe it off with. I looked around the room again as if a second look was going to give me a different outcome. I canceled out all the same possible candidates as before, looked down at my sweatpants, and looked at the mess caused by my sweatpants' inability to effectively clean anything. Not wanting to go through that whole charade again, I began licking my jar of honey.

This was me cleaning.

"Really, JJ," I said to myself as I realized what I was doing. "Thirty? Is this what thirty-year-olds do when they make a mess?"

What *do* thirty-year-olds do when they make a mess? Do thirty-year-olds even make messes? I'm sure they at least have paper towels.

So you can see, I don't feel like an adult. I don't feel like I'm thirty. I have eight months of experience being thirty, and while it might seem like I should be further along in having this thirty-year-old stuff figured out, especially since I'm only heading into more thirties, in the grand scheme of things eight months isn't a lot of time.

I was twenty-eight years old when I was first told about my parents separating. Up to that point, I had twenty-eight years of experience being the by-product of a married couple. And sure, my parents would say I was more to them than a mere by-product of their relationship, but for fact's sake, my frame of reference for *twenty-eight years* had been from the standpoint of a kid whose parents, maybe not always happy, were nonetheless married.

Twenty-eight years later, whether I liked it or not, I was handed a new frame of reference, a new identity, so to speak, without any experience in the field I now found myself living in. And somewhere along the way, I told myself I had better figure out quickly how to stand in this new frame of reference and how to carry myself as the by-product of an expired relationship.

I don't know why I expect myself to have everything figured out all the time. I don't know why I expect myself to just get over it without ever really dealing with it, "it" being a number of things. In my efforts to "just be okay" with everything over the last few years, I have ended up not being okay with anything.

The truth is, I'm two years in as a kid with separated parents and less than a year in as a kid with divorced parents; and while the separation may have given me a heads-up as to what was coming, it didn't prepare me for the emotions that came with the finality of divorce. Having a warning sign of hard roads ahead doesn't lessen the sting of the hardship. When I was eleven, I knew my grandmother was dying of cancer. Knowing she was going to die one day, as we all do, didn't ease any sort of pain the day she actually died. I wasn't shocked that she died; I was shocked that it still hurt as much as it did while having known it was going to happen.

And so it goes with my family. Two years ago I was given a heads-up, a means by which to prepare myself for what lay ahead; and two years later, I'm still shocked by the pain of how much it hurts.

I can't figure out how to get over my parents separating in two years any more than I can figure out how to make thirty look good in eight months. I have spent a lot of time trying to appear okay on the surface, and while I do think there is something to be said for carrying yourself well, there is a fine line between playing a poor hand well and bluffing your way through the entire game. Wanting to appear okay without actually being okay has wasted a lot of time of actually being okay. And I'd rather be okay than look okay because I barely even shower as it is, so I don't know who I think I'm kidding with the whole looking-okay thing.

And the beautiful thing about all the mess I find myself in is how beautiful life really is ... even in, almost especially in, the midst of heartache. It is as I have allowed myself to grieve that I have been able to experience and notice the simplest of details I've often overlooked or bypassed quickly when things were "just fine." If everything was just fine all the time, then nothing would ever be great, glorious, or even miraculous. I think life would be quite boring, if not horrible, if everything was just fine all the time. The sunset would be no big deal, the sunrise would be no surprise, the smell of flowers would offer no hope that spring is in fact coming, and the hope for spring or a new season in general would cease to exist, since there would be no need for hope if everything was always "just fine."

I lay in my bed the other day and cried. Perhaps that's a sad story to some, a sentence I should keep to myself since it's not an attractive quality for a thirty-year-old woman to say she lies in her bed and cries. But like I said, I'm only eight months in as a thirty-year-old, and not only is that *not* the end of the story; it's not the only side of it.

The other side of the story is the one in which I get up and get out of bed. I wash my face, put on a jacket and some shoes, grab my keys and headphones, and head outside. I walk past the beautiful duck pond where I live, quack at the ducks in an attempt to say hi, and walk out onto the street, which is going to lead me to the house of some dear friends. As I walk, I take in the smell of the flowers, the dogwood trees, and the magnolia trees. I thank God for new life and second chances. I look at the color I am surrounded by, knowing much of Oregon's gorgeous color has much to do with the rain we endure all year. I thank God for the color, I thank God for the rain, and I thank God it is not raining that day.

I hit play on my iPod, and there Patty Griffin sings in my ears but straight to my soul.

"Oh, heavenly day..." I'd repeat it all if I could but I don't know how copyrights work, and as an artist I know they are important, even if I don't know how or why. Nonetheless, I highly recommend you listen to Patty Griffin's song *Heavenly Day* and cry along... or sing along.

The song makes me smile, the trees make me smile, and the smell of the flowers makes me smile. The fact that I am not crying makes me smile; and overwhelmed by all the beauty I am surrounded by, embracing the moment in which I find the day to be heavenly, I start running in excitement over nothing in particular, just at the mere thought of being able to see, smell, run, and be alive.

As I ran, I danced and slapped trees and plants, giving high fives to rosemary bushes as if they were spectators at a race, cheering me on to live life well.

For a moment I thought about how weird I might look running while dancing and high-fiving rosemary bushes, but then I looked up, and there in all its glory was a sign that said, KEEP PORTLAND WEIRD. I had never felt more normal, and I laughed aloud as I ran harder, borrowing what time I had in that moment not to have a care in the world about anything less than what God deemed beautiful, and His view of beauty overwhelmed me.

So there is that side of the story as well, the side that looks as heavenly as I can wrap my head around the concept of heaven to be, and even that isn't the only other side of the story; there are many sides involving friends and strangers and, as hard as it might be sometimes, family. I don't tell the side of the story in which I allow myself to lie in bed and cry as a means for someone to feel sorry for me; that's only one side of the story. I tell it because I find that side of the story to be just as important as all the other sides.

As I went to bed that night without Patty Griffin in my ears, I cried again. Different sides of the story can surface and resurface multiple times, sometimes three or four times over in one day, but I think that is okay since I think it is all part of the process. I cried about what hurt, and I let it hurt. I began to bury my face in my hands as I sobbed. I took a deep breath, and as I breathed in, all I could smell was rosemary.

My crying turned into laughing as I thought about running and dancing and rosemary high fives. I held on to the joy of those moments with the evidence of such joy being real still lingering on my hands.

My story isn't over yet, and neither is yours; nor will those stories ever really be over on this side of eternity. And even on the other side of eternity, I don't think our stories will be over, but they will be starting anew, dancing and celebrating for an infinite duration of time. I love to dance, and I believe God loves to watch us dance, be that literally or figuratively, and it is probably because I believe this that I sometimes try to dance prematurely, if there is such a thing. "You have turned my mourning into joyful dancing," David said in Psalm 30:11.

"Let's skip that mourning part," I sometimes say, "and just dance." And while that certainly can be done, there is something to be said for dancing after mourning, for being moved into a place of dancing as a result of having overcome something difficult. Coming out victorious after a long and strenuous battle allows one to dance in a way that they never could have while trying to skip over the tough stuff. Celebratory dancing is the best kind of dancing.

Dancing *because of* and not *instead of* is my favorite kind of dancing. As I have allowed myself to feel the pain of the last few years and realize I can survive the pain, I feel set free from the fear of the pain, and I dance more freely.

Yes, at thirty years old, I still cry under my covers sometimes. Perhaps that is my spade to reveal, a simple fact I like to hide: I am an undercover crier. But make no mistake that I know how to rip those covers right off and dance like nobody is watching.

"Thank You, Lord," I said aloud as I was going to bed that night, smelling the joy of that day while wiping tears from my eyes. "Thank You, thank You ... for turning my mourning into dancing and for rosemary high fives."

Life is hard. Dance harder.

Goodbye for Now

I don't know how to feel about Xuni dying. It doesn't feel real. Xuni was never supposed to die. I mean, we're all supposed to die but not Xuni. Somehow she was oddly immortal to me, perhaps because she seemed so unlike the human race I have experienced.

As a Christian I felt the pressure to share God with her. As a person I just wanted to have the freedom to hang out with her, love her, and learn from her without having to think of her as a project. She wasn't a project, if for no other reason than that she seemed more like Jesus than most Christians I knew, myself included.

I couldn't quite figure out how to tell someone they "needed Jesus" when the person seemed more like Jesus than I did. I couldn't quite figure out how to tell someone they needed a God that at the time I was usually mad at but about whom I knew I was supposed to tell people. Because of the pressure I felt (presumably from God) to tell people how great He was and how much they needed Him, the less I wanted to talk about God.

Most of the time I was mad at God (especially the God of the Old Testament), and so most of the time I went over to Xuni's to feel free from religion, and together we painted or built things with wood, and I learned from her how to love people. I learned how to love people from

Xuni—not because she told me how but because I watched her do it. I watched her love people, no matter who they were—the mailman, the yard guys, the annoying neighbor who let her kids run rampant in Xuni's yard and mine. Xuni loved them.

We shared tea in the afternoons while her half-blind and half-deaf cats tried to make their way around the kitchen, often running into the cabinets. Nine months out of the year, Xuni had a fire going in her wood-burning stove. In the winter months, Xuni and I stayed inside and painted. Sometimes we collaborated on art pieces, and sometimes we each did our own thing. I put on Sam Cooke, and she made us something hot to drink, along with something sweet, and we painted. Sometimes we talked, sometimes we sat in silence, but we always sat together, tucked away in her corner room, painting whatever came to mind.

She hated goodbyes because they seemed too final, so whether I left her house for the day or we'd get off the phone, she always sent me off with "Goodbye for now." She said doing this took away any anxiety about not knowing when she'd see people again. "You never know," she said.

I remember the first time I went to Xuni's house to paint. I was intimidated in part because she was an excellent painter, and my insecurity almost kept me from letting her ever see anything I had to paint, and in other part because she had a semi-large skeleton hanging from the window of her front room. She was fascinated by life and death and the process and transition from life to death. She was also fascinated by the human body and the wonder it all was and is, so in all of her fascination and appreciation for the gift of life contained within a human body, she had a real skeleton hanging in her living room year round as an art piece.

Xuni was a weird one, and I say that only because she would be the first to proudly say it about herself. So she was a weird one, but she was a good weird one. Xuni was in her fifties, but if you had to guess, you would most certainly have guessed late thirties. She was as all naturally beautiful as one could get. With never a hint of makeup and often a genuine smile on her face, she remains one of the most beautiful women I have ever known.

In the spring and summer, Xuni and I spent time outside, working on our gardens. Xuni taught me about flowers and growing vegetables. Mine were never as good as hers, but I never felt like mine needed to be as good as hers; I just felt like I wanted to learn more from her. Xuni taught me how to build a flower box, and I built my first one under her supervision. I would bring pounds of coffee grounds back from work for us to use to "perk up the garden," as Xuni would say. She taught me about sprouts and took me to the "sprout store" to get my own setup for growing my own sprouts in a jar. Occasionally Xuni and I had to locate a chicken around the neighborhood that had flown the coop from her backyard.

Xuni was as in touch with nature and life found within it as she was with people and life found within them. She believed in leading ants outside as opposed to killing them. I didn't know how someone could lead ants outside, but Xuni did.

She taught me the importance of asking, a hard thing for an insecure girl to do. I was afraid of asking for things because I was afraid of what people would think of me. I was afraid of inconveniencing people, even at the expense of not getting something I needed. I was deeply insecure. Xuni was very much at peace with herself and the world. "A yes you may get, a no you already have if you don't ask," she would say. She allowed me to practice on her by asking her for things I needed or simply just wanted. Every now and then she dropped a swear word in front of a "no" just to show me I could survive a *no* and to show herself she could survive *saying* no. She was a recovering people pleaser who was still trying to practice boundaries with people.

Together we were somewhat of a mess yet beautiful in every way, because we were so in the moment; in each moment we found ourselves. Xuni gave me my first stick-shift lessons in her car, took me to community painting classes, and was the first to instruct me on how to road-trip safely and adventurously. She always shared whatever she had with me; whether it was eggs "fresh from the chicken butt" or an overpriced french pastry, she made sharing seem easy. Sharing was never easy for me, but after spending time with Xuni, I knew I wanted to get better at it. I always felt like I was growing or learning something in her presence. My heart felt happy every time I saw Xuni, as well as challenged, since growing isn't always easy, and seeing what you like in someone else sometimes reveals what you don't like in yourself.

I moved out of our triplex about a year before Xuni did. We kept in touch for a little while with phone calls and after a while not so much unless I occasionally stopped by. Eventually she moved out too, and I knew our season of life together was coming to a close, not because either of us wanted it to but simply because seasons change and sometimes people move. She had always dreamed of living on a farm, and she moved out of our triplex into her dream on a farm outside Portland, where her chickens could run freely, and I'm sure she could too.

A few years have gone by since I saw Xuni last. She will forever hold a place in my heart and has shaped a lot of who I've become. She was someone who was much nicer and much more at peace with herself than the sad and angry girl I started out as when I first moved into the triplex. I learned a lot about how to live like Jesus from Xuni because I learned a lot about how to take care of myself, freeing me up to genuinely love other people. I learned how to take what I had read about in scripture and live it out in the world.

Xuni gave me the freedom to be me, never once trying to convince me to believe what she believed about life or God. Never once did she put me down for what I believed about life or God. She loved me for who I was, differences and all, and I knew this to be true the day we stumbled into an antique shop together and got into a conversation with the man who ran the shop. He made a remark about "those crazy Christians," and Xuni lovingly and patiently said, "Not all Christians are crazy." Then she looked at me and winked.

Xuni defended the person, not the faith, but that person had a faith that by default challenged the stereotype against that faith. "Most Christians are crazy though," I said, and we laughed as I stored the golden nugget of that experience in the pockets of my mind. In feeling defended by someone of a different faith, I felt like a person, not a project. I knew Xuni loved me, but there was something in that moment that made me feel loved without agenda. This opened my eyes to see just how much I had loved people *with* an agenda, making me wonder how much I had really loved people at all.

My best friend, Anna, called me yesterday to tell me Xuni had died. I'm finding it hard to say much past that news. It didn't feel real. I couldn't wrap my head around it. I still can't. Even though we hadn't seen each other in a while, she was always supposed to be there; there was always supposed to be time to spend with her again. I was supposed to go out to the farm and run around with her and the chickens, pick vegetables, drink tea, and paint. In my mind Xuni was always going to be there. I'm thankful for the memories we have, but I don't want that to be it. I don't want only a box of memories.

I want to know I can still open that box and crawl back in and relive our time together. It wasn't supposed to be this way. She was too young and too full of life and love she was so willing to share that it doesn't make sense to me for her to die. Anna told me it was a brain tumor, but I just don't understand. I know death happens all the time to people all over the world and sometimes under the most bizarre and unjust circumstances, and I can so easily chalk it up to life not being fair; but the closer it hits to home, the harder it becomes to be so nonchalant about life and death not being fair.

I cried the second Anna's news came out of her mouth. I couldn't hold it in; it all just came pouring out of me. I kept saying I didn't understand; it seemed to be the only thing I could get out of my mouth, the only thing I could even wrap my head around—the fact that I didn't understand. I still don't. Nothing about life seems fair when someone you love dies, especially when you claim to believe in an afterlife that may or may not involve them depending on what you or they believed. None of it makes sense, and I don't understand it. Sometimes I don't even understand what I believe, especially when someone dies, someone I love, someone I was "supposed" to convert according to my faith. But then I have to ask myself about my faith and what I believe.

Do I actually believe the perfect sentence structure of a certain prayer is going to be what saves people from hell? Do I actually believe this life is about avoiding hell and trying to get other people to avoid it, too? I believe hell is real, not so much as a fiery furnace and a devil running around with a pitchfork but certainly as a state of being in which you are separated from the presence of God—a state of being in which I would never want to find myself nor wish upon anyone else. Based on that fact, I guess I am avoiding hell and wanting other people to avoid it too. But avoiding hell isn't the driving force of my life; it's more of a by-product in desiring God's presence and wanting to chill with Him instead of without Him.

Xuni loved Jesus. I think, like most of us, she had a hard time with people who claimed to follow Jesus but lived contrary to what Jesus was about. I have a hard time with those people, which means I have a hard time with myself. My time with Xuni may not have looked like a prescription for Christianity, but it was honest and real, and I told her that, for as much as I didn't understand life and people, I knew I loved Jesus, and I wanted to be about what He was about, even if it was hard. I think I was struggling so much in that season of life because I was learning that it was hard to follow Jesus. It's hard to go against the norm and not be part of the in crowd, so I was confused a lot because I thought following Jesus was supposed to be easier, and maybe I was doing it wrong.

On top of that, so many Christians I knew lived how they wanted and slapped grace on their behavior, which looked nothing like the Jesus I read about. And I get it—there is grace, there is always grace, and believe me, I will be the first to line up and be thankful for grace. But there's also something to be said for encountering Jesus and changing our self-destructive ways as a result of having encountered Him.

I think a lot of people work their way to Jesus, and when they get tired of doing all their good works, they burn out, they give up, and they make choices that hurt themselves and others. Then they feel bad about it, reach for grace, ask for forgiveness, and repeat the cycle. Many people don't chill long enough to get to know Jesus. They get tired before they even get to Him, causing a lot of unrest and chaos in their lives. I speak for myself.

There's a lot I don't know, but I know that in many ways, more than most, Xuni lived like Jesus, and the way she lived her life spoke louder than a sermon with no follow-through. From doing life with Xuni, I learned to speak less and live more. I learned to let my actions speak for me, to actually love people instead of talking about the importance of loving people. I learned to shake the pressure off my shoulders, as well as the devil off my back, and I learned to dance in the freedom of being me, at least for a few short moments during a really hard season. I still kill ants, but I apologize when doing so if for no other reason than to acknowledge life when I see it.

We are not only in life. We are surrounded by life; it's everywhere. The afterlife isn't even a thing that happens after life. It's still life, just in a new and different way, a more perfect, less painful kind of way. At least I think so. When I pray, "On earth as it is in heaven," I ask God what that looks like for me to play a part in bringing heaven to earth, not "when the world ends" but here and now. If eternity really does mean forever, then we are already in it, and we don't have to wait for earth to be like heaven. Perhaps in some ways over things we can't control but in things we can control, like sharing, making eye contact, smiling, buying someone a cup of coffee, not stealing when it would be oh so easy and overlooked. In each of these little moments, we all contribute to making earth as it is in heaven. Xuni did that. I truly believe Xuni treated the earth as if it were heaven, not just because she saved the trees and the wildlife but because she saved people from the lie that they weren't lovable.

People are loved whether on earth or in heaven, if heaven is some distant place. The difference (I think) is that people in heaven *know* they are loved, and they live out of that truth. While she was on earth, Xuni helped people know they were loved by loving them, no matter what their story. Xuni played a part in heaven touching earth, and she did the will of the Father as a result of how she lived her life.

My heart hurts and aches over the thought of her not walking this earth anymore, and for now that is where I am, knowing it is good to grieve and loving myself (as Xuni taught me to do) by allowing myself to do so.

Xuni, my friend, goodbye for now.

A Bottle of Change

It was September. I stood at the bottom of our creaky wooden stairs in our cold Portland home, trying to figure out how I was going to pay rent. Liz came out of her room from across where I was standing and told me she had something for me. "I've felt like I was supposed to give this to you for a few weeks, but I thought it was stupid. I've been praying for you, and the only thing I've been hearing back is to give this to you. I keep saying, 'No, God, that's dumb,' but He keeps telling me to give it to you." I laughed as she said all this to me, wondering what it could possibly be. She pulled from behind her back a large plastic bottle of change.

"I've been saving this for years," she said. "I don't know what for, and I know it's not much or what you could even do with it, but I think I'm supposed to give it to you."

While it might have "just" been a bottle of change, I knew it represented something greater. It represented a woman giving what little she had in the support of a friend. It represented obedience when it didn't make sense. It represented provision at a time of questioning and uncertainty. The bottle of change wasn't going to pay my rent, but that wasn't the point; and if I had focused on that being the point, of still being without, I would have missed what God was doing altogether. I would have missed an entire season of life I now have locked up in the treasure chest of my heart and mind.

The bottle of change was the change I was looking for in my life that I didn't know I needed. Prior to that morning at the bottom of the stairs, I had been stagnant, confused, heart-broken and on the verge of further entertaining my apathy to settle for a less-than version of life ... one of survival and just barely getting by. This is a place where I have found myself more than once in life, and since life comes in waves, I think I'd be a fool to say it will never happen again.

August had ended poorly with a blowout fight in my front yard with the man I thought I was going to marry one day. I was blindsided after he told me he was still in love with his ex-girlfriend. I loaded his belongings into a large camping cooler and dropped it at his feet. He threw it in the back of his truck and drove off. There was no resolve or well-wishes, only confusion and arguing with an abrupt finish; and just like that, as if the last year of ups and downs and ins and outs held no weight, the relationship was over.

I knew I wanted to write for a living, but I felt stuck. I often feel stuck when it comes to writing. I think it's part of the process. There's so much I want to say and so much that happens in between finding the right words to say and finding the right time to express those words that it all gets jammed up inside my head and sticks together like glue. I end up having a paper-mache ball of thoughts that tumble around in my insides and make me feel crazy until I get them out. I felt crazy in part because I still didn't fully understand what had happened that day in my front yard and in part because I had a bounty of sticky thoughts tumbling around in my insides and I couldn't get them out.

I put the bottle of change under my desk for safekeeping, unsure what I was going to use it for but extremely grateful for the act of love and kindness my roommate had shown me.

One morning while I was trying to write, my foot kicked something under my desk, and I heard the change rattle. "What do you want me to do with that change?" I asked God. I felt like there was a reason God had wanted Liz to give it to me, but I didn't know what to do with it. I can't say He spoke clearly or audibly, but I felt like the response was simple, almost too simple, like there was no way *that* was why I had been given the bottle of change. "Go get coffee."

I'm an early-morning person, so I decided that next morning I would get coffee and try to write at a coffee shop before work. Maybe I just needed a new atmosphere to clear my head. I was working as a cook at a preschool at the time, and seeing as how I needed to be at school by 7:30 a.m. to begin food preparations for the day, I needed to be at the coffee shop by 6 a.m. with the hopes of being there for at least an hour. Portland is littered with coffee shops; sometimes half the battle is just picking somewhere to go. I didn't have a car at the time, so I picked a shop that had the combination of early-morning opening, convenient location, and good coffee.

The following morning I gathered enough change for a cup of coffee, bundled up, and walked to Albina Press on Hawthorne Street. It was quiet, just how I liked it. I scanned the whole place over before deciding on a well-lit seat at the big wooden counter overlooking the rest of the shop. Seating is everything; finding the right spot to sit in a coffee shop is sometimes just as much a battle as finding the right coffee shop. There were a total of four men in the shop, one of them being the barista. Two men sat in the back, one on a couch, and the other at a table. The fourth man sat at the big wooden counter, only a couple of seats down from the seat I had chosen.

The man at the big wooden counter smiled and nodded as I unloaded my things near him. I was clearly a newcomer to a regular's scene. I got a cup of coffee, opened my composition notebook, and began to write out some of the things swirling through my head. I've always said that a good composition notebook makes the best therapist. Even if I've never actually said it to anyone else, I've said it to myself, especially when I'm broke and in need of an emotional unloading.

I returned to Albina Press the next morning and every following morning that work week. Each morning it was the same scene: the two men in the back of the shop, the old man at the big wooden counter. I slept in a little later on the weekend and returned the following week to the early-morning scene at The Albina Press. I returned every morning for the next six months; a cup of coffee each morning was fully funded by the bottle of change my roommate had felt led to give me. I continued to go each morning, even after the bottle of change ran out because, as it turns out, if you stop running from place to place and stick around long enough, you might make some friends ... even a family.

And that is what happened. An odd family was born in the early hours of the morning at Albina Press. We all came for different reasons, but there we all were ... together. Much of what I wrote during that time was about my heartache and the loss of the man I still loved. It was a rough season, but I never felt more alive than when I was at Albina Press, writing out my hurts and pausing to laugh with Uncle Larry, the old man at the big wooden counter.

Larry became Uncle Larry early on in our early-morning friendship, a retired hippie in his late sixties; I was a wanna-be hippie in my early thirties. We were an odd pair to find occupying the big wooden counter together, but there we were faithfully each morning during the week at six o'clock in the morning.

Larry had the best seat, where the hanging lights above hit the counter just right. I took second best just on the outskirts of the light but closer to the outlet on the other side of the counter. I secretly envied Larry's spot, but it was Larry's, so not even on the rare occasion that I beat him to the shop did I have the heart to take it. Come to think of it, I don't think I ever beat Larry to the shop; it didn't cross my mind as being possible seeing as how he got up at 4:30 a.m. every morning to walk and wait for Albina to open. Larry was usually there before I got there; if he wasn't, it was because he was out of town, which was rare. When Larry went out of town, I kept his seat occupied, but other than that, I always sat two seats over, close enough to talk, with enough room for our elbows, as he read the paper and I wrote.

Every so often, the two men sitting in the back came over and talked with us at the big wooden counter; another regular named

Bruce came in on occasion and sat with us. "We got the grumpy old man's club here at the counter," Bruce said one day.

"What about her?" Larry asked. "She ain't grumpy, and she ain't a man!"

Bruce looked me over; it took him a little longer to warm up to me. "She ain't a man, but I bet she has an inner grump." He paused. "And an old soul ... she belongs." He cracked a smile at me.

I had never felt more honored to feel like I belonged somewhere than the grumpy old man's club.

The grumpy old men might have been intimidating to those who weren't part of their group, but once you got in, you realized they were just big, old softies who had seen a lot in life. They'd bicker about politics, poke fun at the baristas (who were always able to poke back), and tell stories about "back in their day" as they observed the oddities of the young folks around them.

I loved the grumpy old men, but Larry and I grew the closest, if for no other reason than our close proximity. It's hard to sum up Larry because Larry was as eclectic and interesting as a person could get. It seemed Larry had been a little bit of everything at some point in his life. From an elementary school principal to the mayor of a small town in the Midwest to a Volkswagen repair man to an antique shop owner and avid mushroom hunter, Larry had lived a full life with a wealth of knowledge. He sported a gray beard and long gray hair, which he always wore in a pony tail.

He did tai chi in his backyard and said his neighbors thought he was weird. He'd laugh and say he knew he was weird and wasn't really sure whether what he did could be considered tai chi. "I'm pretty sure I'm doing it wrong. It might be more like chai tea than tai chi! Chai tea is a thing, right?"

I laughed and affirmed it was a thing. He always commented on the color of pen I was using; I found it humorous that he noticed. I usually wrote in blue or black ink, and then one morning simply because it was the only color I could find, I came in with a red pen.

"Well, looky there!" Larry exclaimed. "She's writing with red today! None of this sad, dark stuff. You must have had a good weekend to come in with a bright-red pen!"

I laughed, and before I could comment, he kept going. "You know, all the important stuff is in red ... I think the Christians put all Jesus's stuff in red ... or maybe Jesus did. I don't know, but I know it's important!"

I told him my sad journal was certainly not as important as the Bible. Larry shrugged. "Maybe it is. You're important." And he smiled as he sipped his coffee.

"You know," Larry said, "we have the same birthday."

"Who does?" I asked.

"Me and Jesus," he said. "I don't mind the guy, but His people are kinda crazy."

I laughed and agreed that it was sad but true.

"Every year on Christmas the shop hangs a sign for me over the counter that says LARRY CHRISTMAS! The Christians get mad and call it blasphemy, but the shop leaves it up anyway. And besides, it's not blasphemy. It's my birthday! I'm pretty sure Jesus is okay if we share the day."

I said I thought He was.

"We all drink whiskey and coffee and hang out here on Christmas morning. You should come this year." I felt happy to be invited and said I would come.

Under Uncle Larry's tutelage (though I doubt he would call it that), I rediscovered an appreciation for the simplest of things in life. He collected feathers and succulent plants, and every so often he placed one on my notebook. He liked only Guatemalan coffee and was passionate about mushrooms. Larry taught me that people are more messed up and more beautiful than we ever thought possible.

My journal started with processing a loss, but it began to be filled with funny and hopeful stories about life, all told by Uncle Larry. At a time when I felt most hurt by a fellow human, another fellow human came along and showed me there was good in life. Even when it was hard, the coffee got cold, and it was time to go to work, there was still good in life.

Most of the time, the good was in the small stuff, like a bottle of change that changes who and where you spend your mornings and how you get through dark seasons. Uncle Larry was crucial to the healing of my heart during that time, something I never would have known or seen coming. I remember coming in one morning and him saying to me, “You know, kid, you’re gonna be okay. I wasn’t so sure when you first started coming in here, but I think you’re gonna be okay.”

We laughed, and I agreed. The emptier the bottle became, the fuller my heart was, and the more it made sense to me that God wanted me to have it.

Every little bit counts, even the smallest of gestures or amount of change.

Coffee without Vows

I keep Abby's address in the front pocket of my backpack. I think about her all the time and even more so about writing her another letter. I keep her address on my person in case I get a break at work or find some time on the train to actually write the letter I always think about writing her. Time goes by so fast; letter writing takes a bit longer.

Abby lives in San Luis Obispo, California, surrounded by vineyards and mountains and really nice neighbors. I met Abby back in 2012 while living out of my car on a road trip around the country. I go back to visit her and her husband, Rob, from time to time; and when not visiting, Abby and I like to keep the postmen and postwomen employed by writing each other letters.

Before meeting Abby, I had lost a bit of hope in people (myself included). I was also new to the "I'm *never* getting married" club and the extremism that came with it. When you grow up and realize "happily ever after" ain't so happy or forever, you begin to lose hope in the whole marriage idea and the people who think it's such a great idea. I thought I was destined for the same story of those I saw around me, especially once my parents' marriage had ended. I was never really a fan of marriage, perhaps because I grew up in a home where my parents didn't want their kids to grow up in a broken home, so they stayed together "for the kids." I get it, but kids sense the brokenness well before the lawyers get involved. I don't know the right answers to dealing with divorce, but I do know that kids are really aware, and validating their reality will always help them in the long run.

Anyway, I grew up and dated someone for seven years, and when that ended, I dated someone for two years. And when that ended, I dated someone for one year. And when that ended, I assumed everything always ended, so I decided I would never get married. Something deep down told me I still wanted marriage, but I usually shut it up with chips and salsa. Problem solved. It was a salty season. Nonetheless, I vowed never to make a vow and figured that would be my last vow. It was a fear-based decision, and I lived by it until three years ago. Until I met Abby.

And so the story goes ...

A guy I had never met over Facebook asked me out for coffee. You know the Facebook drill; we had mutual friends, he saw my picture, and he sent me a message, asking me out to coffee. I thought he was a creeper and showed the message to all my girlfriends. They laughed because they all knew who he was and said we were polar opposites. Fair enough. I'm a creative sort, disorganized, easily distracted, overly emotional, and often irrational. The guy asking me out to coffee was a self-proclaimed type A: organized, focused, rational, and in complete control of his emotions. Truth be told, I was a little intimidated, but whenever I feel that way or find myself comparing myself to someone else, I put my hand on my heart and whisper to myself, "You're rad, too!" It's weird, but it works and takes a lot less time than repeating daily affirmations in the mirror every morning.

I was intrigued but didn't want to be. I didn't want to go out for coffee because I didn't want to get married. I know, that sounds bizarre, but it's a common misunderstanding in the church. Whether it's an extremist thing, a Christian thing, or a girl thing, I learned early on that kissing leads to motherhood, and coffee dates lead to marriage.

I didn't drink coffee until much too late in life. The kissing thing is another story, but I digress.

I think the church is working on addressing that whole issue so guys won't be so scared to ask girls out, and girls won't be so scared to say yes. But if there was even a chance of a coffee date equating to marriage, I just simply wasn't ready.

"Well," one of my girlfriends said, "he's a nice guy, and if nothing else, it could make for a good story!"

That's really all you have to say to get me to do anything. I love a good story, and I'm relatively poor, so based on those two factors, I accepted his invitation.

We went to coffee, and we laughed, and he asked good questions and was nice to the waitress, and I felt happy. It was a great date with a mediocre cup of coffee and a side order of yams. He called later that week and asked whether he could make me my favorite breakfast: biscuits and gravy. Who says no to that?

Long story short, we didn't get married. Mainly because while he was in the middle of making the biscuits, I told him I didn't want to get married (mind you, he didn't ask). While I enjoyed his company, I knew I wasn't interested. In part because he wasn't my type (literally, I'm not a type A) but mostly because, if I'm calling a spade a spade and not pretending to be tough and disinterested, I was terrified. Because of my vow never to make vows, I didn't want to keep being treated so well and "fooled" into thinking a relationship could not only work but *last*. In retrospect I realize that sounds extreme, but as the recovering extremist I am, I didn't want to entertain a relationship if it was destined for a dead end. It was the first time I realized what my view of marriage had become: a dead end.

Not wanting to keep using him for free coffee or to leave him hanging to figure it all out, I told him upfront the second time we hung out (not the best timing, but what did I know?). I told him I wasn't interested in pursuing anything past friendship. I even told him why. And maybe he thought I was crazy, but he respected and appreciated my honesty, and because of that we stayed on good terms, maintaining our friendship from a safe distance. No more mediocre coffee, no more side order of yams, no more biscuits and gravy and enjoying good company in fear of where it might go.

The following summer I was fired from my job as a flight attendant due to an unfair customer complaint with no chance to explain what had happened. Apparently the customer is always right, even when she isn't (because she wasn't). I think I felt betrayed by life, like nothing was turning out the way I had thought it would. I didn't realize life worked like that until my parents divorced *and* my relationship ended *and* I lost my job. I think I was on the verge of having a breakdown while still managing to smile everywhere I went. I decided to sell all my stuff, fit what I could in my car, and just start driving. I wish I would have saved my CD player, but other than that, I'm pretty okay with everything I sold. My "drive" turned into a two-month soul-searching road trip around the country.

I drove and cried and prayed and healed from a lot of stuff that had been bottled up over the years. I faced myself in the emptiness of my car by day and enjoyed the company of people I stayed with by night. I usually cried myself to sleep because I was sad, and I usually cried when I drove because I thought everything was so beautiful. It was an emotional trip. People who "followed" that journey and saw pictures kept commenting on what a fun adventure I was on; and I was, but I was also experiencing the dark night of the soul night after night, feeling the pain I had been avoiding for so long.

I needed somewhere to stay between San Francisco and Los Angeles, and I racked my brain for options so I wouldn't have to sleep in my car again. While most of me was healing, some of me was going a little crazy. I remembered that my coffee date, now "friend at a safe distance" (insert face-plant emoji), had contacts in San Luis Obispo. I contacted him and said I'd be passing through and asked whether there was anyone he could connect me with. "YES!" he texted back. "My parents!"

I was hesitant but also desperate, so I texted back, "That'd be great!" You can't really afford to be hesitant when you're desperate and recently unemployed while driving solo around the country, crying most of the way.

My plan was to crash on their couch for one night and head out the next morning, and it was a great plan, except for one thing. I fell in love with his parents. I ended up staying with Rob and Abby for three days, partly because they had a whole bedroom prepared for me but mostly because they had a marriage the likes of which I had never seen, and I was fascinated. For three days I enjoyed their company and learned a lot about commitment and kindness and the importance of the little things, like calling someone "sweetie." I know three days aren't a lot of time to make a judgment call, but everyone has always said things to me like, "When you know, you *know*," and I always hated that ... until I met Rob and Abby, and I just *knew* they had something good.

While staying with Abby and her sweetie, their son sent me a list of everything I had to see while I was in his hometown, specifically the sand dunes since they were "the most beautiful place in the world," according to him. I took notes about where to go, but I'm not really sure what I did with the notes because this was the last thing I recorded on that visit:

> I know this is a beautiful town with lots to do, but it's been very healing for me to just hang around the house with Rob & Abby. I've really enjoyed them. The simplicity of being in their presence stirs something in me as much as the sights of the California coastline but in a much different way. I don't want this trip to only be about beautiful sights. I want it to be about people too. That's why I feel content just being at the house with them, watching them together, the way they talk to each other, look at each other, knowing they still look at each other like that after thirty-plus years. Even if it's small, it does restore some hope in my view of people, but more specifically, it restores some hope in my view

> of marriage. Beautiful views of the ocean can't really do that.

At the end of the three days, my former coffee date asked me whether I had gotten to see everything he recommended. I said no, that I hadn't seen any of it. He was so annoyed and frustrated. "HOW? WHY? What have you been doing!?" he asked.

"Actually I've mostly just been hanging out with your parents," I said.

He sounded even more frustrated. "WHAT!?" he yelled. "Don't get me wrong, I love my parents, but HOW, *HOW* can you be in one of the most beautiful places in the world and not go see it? That's crazy! You're right there!"

The answer was easy.

I had lived the last twenty-eight years of my life with a poor view of marriage, making fear-based decisions in almost every other area of life because of it. And then randomly I had been given a three-day window to look through and see a *different story* … a story of another married couple who not only loved each other through the thick and thin of life but also did *well* by each other, even when life and love got hard. It was the first time I realized that I didn't have to have the same story as my parents (I'm a late learner), that marriage can be hard; but it doesn't have to be a dead end, and I don't have to be afraid. "That's a sight that no sand dune on this earth could ever replace."

"Oh," he said. "Oh okay, yea, that's fair."

I've been back to visit Rob and Abby twice since that trip, and I have yet to see the sand dunes; I know I will eventually, but their company revives something in my spirit and my suspicion that people really are good, so I'm okay just hanging out in their living room, drinking tea, and eating animal crackers. When people say, "God works in mysterious ways," I think that's less about a nice reason for our suffering and more about just how small the thing can be that starts to make us feel a little bit better (even in the midst of our suffering). When people say, "God is in everything," I think that's true, from the sand dunes to the animal crackers. He's in all of it, and that to me is mysterious.

That is why I keep Abby's address on my person three years later. Sometimes I forget what I learned at her feet about commitment and kindness and the importance of calling someone "sweetie," and sometimes I need to be reminded, so we write letters.

Saying yes to that cup of coffee didn't lead to marriage, but it led to a view of marriage that began to heal the one I had and set me free to face my fears, heal old wounds, and find peace in the different way my life is turning out. Whether I ever get married or not, fear won't make the decision for me, and I can enjoy the simplicity of coffee without vows … for now.

The Lunch Lady

April 30, 2014

Today is my last day of work as the lunch lady for an amazing group of preschoolers. I woke up early this morning to write a letter to my kids I'm sure they won't necessarily be able to grasp now, but I wanted to publish it here as a place for them to always come back and find it should they ever forget who they are and how much they are loved.

Earlier in the year, I was mad at the preschoolers for being preschoolers but only because I had gotten to the point of not liking my job, and they were the faces of my job. I think that's when you know it's time to go—when you get mad at preschoolers for being preschoolers. I'm not mad at them anymore, but it took me taking care of myself to stop feeling sorry for myself. With self-pity out of the way as I took ownership of my life and my choices, I could see the preschoolers more clearly, and they really are quite amazing.

This morning I'm going to take my last walk to work where I will fix my last lunch and hear, "Thank you, Ms. JJ" from that amazing group of preschoolers one last time. I hope they grow up to read this letter one day.

Hello My Little Friends,

As you know but may not have added up, I have been your lunch lady for the last year and three months. The time has come for me to say goodbye to you all as I set off for some new adventures in my life, but I wanted to be able to tell you all how much I love you, how much I will miss you, and how much life you have to offer this world.

You are currently in preschool. You're short, you're cute, and you have a whole world and a long life ahead of you. I have never addressed an audience this young, so bear with me as I try and figure out how to relay a message about life that involves a lot of beauty and a lot of scrapped knees and things gone missing, like toys and playmates who might move away and all your baby teeth. Has anyone told you yet that you will lose all the teeth that are currently in your mouth? You will, and it may be easy, or it may be hard, but don't worry. You'll get much better and stronger teeth in return, more durable for the long road ahead.

Life is going to be a lot of that—things gone missing and getting found again and lost again and found again and sometimes not found again but sometimes replaced with something better. It's okay to cry when things go missing. Crying is okay and very necessary; don't ever let anyone tell you not to cry. There are so many things in life worth crying over, so many things that hurt our feelings or bruise our elbows. And when we feel hurt, it is most certainly okay to cry. And crying doesn't just have to happen when you are sad. Sometimes I cry simply because the sky is so beautiful, and smiling just doesn't seem to cut it. Sometimes I laugh so hard I cry. Sometimes crying makes me just as happy as not crying, so I say to you, dear boys and girls, "It is okay for you to cry." Plus, you never really grow up enough to grow out of crying, so you might as well learn to embrace it. To embrace it means to welcome it in your arms and give it a big ol' hug as you learn to love who you are, how you were made, and the emotions you were given.

So there's that—crying is okay.

And there's also this—you all have the most beautiful smiles! I'm back to crying again as I think about each one. Some of them are bright red. Others are a lighter pink. Some are crooked with character, and some are straight as can be. I usually see them covered in food, which quite honestly is one of my favorite ways to see them as you enjoy the food I make for you. But whether drenched in spaghetti sauce, hidden behind chocolate, or clean as a whistle, I love seeing you smile. A smile is a language in and of itself as everyone you meet in life, no matter where they come from; no matter how different they look from you, everyone understands what a smile means. This makes a smile a very powerful thing. Some of you already know this as you try to smile your way out of trouble, so while I say use smiles often, be careful with them. Smiles may get you out of trouble, but not learning a lesson is way worse than getting in trouble, I promise. Oh, and girls, smiling is way better than makeup. No amount of makeup can make you look half as pretty as having a genuine smile on your face. I promise that too.

You should know that much like the lunchroom, life is going to get messy. Life is full of messes. We can clean up real good and wash our hands and brush our teeth and change into a clean pair of pajamas and maybe even have some sweet dreams, but each day is different, and some of those days are going to look squeaky clean, and some of those days are going to look messier than your toy box exploding in your bedrooms. While I don't advise going about and trying to create messes in life, you can certainly expect some messes, even embrace them (remember that hug thing) and still enjoy the life you've been given.

Somewhere along our journey together, me as your lunch lady and you as the precious little mouths I feed, I forgot that life could get messy, especially in the kitchen, and I forgot what life was about as I tried to cover up my messes instead of cleaning them up. Cleaning up a mess is much better than covering it up, I promise. Thank God for Ms. Mackenzie, who came in to help me do the dishes and clean up all the messes I made on my own but would have never been able to clean up without help. Know that it's always okay to ask for help; no mess is too much for someone who loves you to step in and help you. Try your best to hold onto people who aren't afraid of your messes; they are few and far between (that means hard to find). Be sure to say thank you when someone steps in to help you clean up. I shall set that example for you by saying thank you to Ms. Mackenzie now.

Thank you, Ms. Mackenzie, so very much, for stepping in, for lending a helping hand, and for not being afraid to take on my messes. You are more beautiful than you know and not just because you help clean up after me.

So remember, life is messy, but with just the right cleaning crew, it can and will be oh so fun. Ask for help and say thank you. I so hope you all learn to write, since a handwritten thank-you card is one of the best gifts to give and receive. Remember how I said smiles were powerful? So is saying thank you. I will never forget the sound of you all screaming "THANK YOU, MS. JJ!" just before I was about to wonder whether all the work I did in the kitchen was worth it. Let me tell you now that every ounce of effort I put into creating your lunch was worth your smiles and the sound of your voices yelling thank you.

I wish I could wrap your little and brilliant minds around just how much I am going to miss you. It wasn't an easy decision for me to make to leave The Sunshine School, but Ms. JJ needed to take care of herself, which meant she needed to step out of the kitchen for a while. You see, I forgot some very important things along the way, but the most important thing I forgot affected me the most, and I want to share it with you to store in your pockets and purses to maybe pull out and look at somewhere along your own journeys.

I forgot that life isn't about being the prettiest or the coolest. I forgot that for as cool as Spider-Man is and as beautiful as Cinderella is, life is not about being a superhero or a princess. I forgot that while I love my best friend, life isn't about saving a seat for my best friend only to leave someone else out. I forgot that life isn't about being the king of the mountain or the queen of the castle. I forgot that making pretty food doesn't make me have a pretty heart, and saying,

"Look what I can do" never feels as good as saying, "Look what you can do."

I lost sight somewhere along the way, and I forgot about what I think most of life is all about ...

Jesus.

I think life was and is and always will be about Jesus, whether we remember it or not, so I find it most helpful to try to remember. My heart was sad for a long time, simply because I forgot about Jesus, so that is what I hope you remember more than anything else. More than your sandwiches that looked like faces, more than Ms. JJ dancing in the kitchen or the puppet who has surfaced in our last few days together, I hope you always remember who Jesus is.

Jesus saved Ms. JJ at a time when she needed Him most, at a time when her mess seemed too big to clean up, and He rounded up a cleaning crew and got to work. Life is about Jesus. And because life is about Jesus, that means life is about people, because Jesus is about people. The best way to love Jesus is to love yourself (because you are a people) and to love other people, to invite them to sit next to you, to help them clean up, to smile at them, to say thank you.

My heart is excited and heavy as I think about you all going out into this world. My prayer more than anything is that you would know you are loved. You are so deeply loved. Knowing whether we are loved shapes a lot of who we are and how we treat people, so the simplest way I can think to pray that you would never forget Jesus is to pray that you would never forget how loved you are.

I'm quite sure your attention spans haven't held out this long. Perhaps I should have addressed the Jesus thing first, but perhaps one day when you are older, you can come back and read this letter and be reminded of the time you spent in a place called Lunch Lady Land within the county lines of The Sunshine School. Perhaps you can be reminded of how good your food was but more importantly how much your lunch lady loved you—but even more importantly how much Jesus still loves you no matter what you've done, no matter what road you've taken, no matter what age you come back and read this letter.

Though I am not ready to think about not seeing your faces every morning, the time comes in all of our lives to take the next road. Kindergarten is soon ahead of you, so our ways would have parted soon enough anyhow. I've never been good at saying goodbyes, and so I used to avoid them, but I'm learning that you just never really know what life brings you, which sometimes includes bringing something back you thought you had to say goodbye to. So this isn't goodbye, at least not forever, because who knows when and where we might see each other again, be it at the grocery store in a few weeks or ten years down the road after I've written a book a two. Did I tell you that yet? I want to write books and tell stories ... and make no mistake that my time spent with all of you helped shape that. And because some of you have already started asking, yes, I am going to cook for myself at home.

So cry when you need to, laugh a lot, smile big, get dirty, hug the mess, but don't leave it there. Find a good cleaning crew, ask for help, say thank you, be nice to people, be willing to give up your seat, nourish those little bodies with lots of good food, be a kid as long as you can, but don't ever be afraid to get older (adulthood isn't as scary as I thought it would be). Love each other, love your teachers, love your parents and guardians, love people, let Jesus love you, and never, ever, ever give up.

Life is worth every bit of breath you have. Even on the toughest of days and the most sleepless of nights, life is so incredibly beautiful. Don't let it pass you by, live it up, and live it well. It is with great appreciation for my time spent with you that I say goodbye for now. I love you, my little friends. I really, really love you.

With much love and much muchness, your lunch lady, Ms. JJ

Part 2

Lunch Lady Land, as I came to call it after one of my favorite Saturday Night Live skits, came to an end in April of 2014. I had spent the last year and a half crafting food into art and making sandwiches look like anything but food. My goal was to never make a sandwich *just* a sandwich and work to the best of my ability. I fulfilled that goal and added food art to my portfolio, even if it did slowly become my own worst enemy in the process. I finished well and went out on top. On my last day, I made chicken pot pies with messages written to the kids in the top layer of the crust. You can still view them on Facebook if you look up the "lunch lady" and find the right one.

Lunch Lady Land wasn't the only thing that came to an end in the beginning months of 2014. In the midst of quitting my job and with my parents' divorce freshly final, I was also in the process of ending a long-term on-again, off-again relationship—a relationship I so desperately wanted to work out; hence the on again after the off agains. I believe the expression is "When it rains, it pours." It felt as though my identity was slowly slipping out of my fingers, and I was flailing.

I had been in the process of looking for other jobs, not aggressively but enough not to appear irresponsible. As a Christian, I find there is a fine line between being irresponsible and trusting a God who does crazy things, especially when you are in your thirties. There are voices that have told me to grow up well before I hit thirty, but there was something about hitting thirty that skyrocketed that piece of advice—to just grow up and get serious. I have wrestled and wrestled and wrestled over this piece of advice. Why does quitting my job mean I'm not serious? The disciples gave up everything they had to follow a homeless man … really?

One fateful morning, when I was trying to figure out how to fit into this world as the (self-proclaimed) unique individual God had created me to be, I logged onto Facebook after being on a social media hiatus for over a year. The very first post I saw was by a guy I had met on a road trip in 2012. His post said, "Anyone interested in a paid internship working with high schoolers at a church in San Diego for the summer? Message me for details." So I did.

On my last day of work as the lunch lady, I found out I had gotten the job as the youth group intern in San Diego. I accepted and walked away from having a salary to being an intern—every mother's dream for her adult child.

And so began the season of life in which I set about to pursue writing while leaving the comforts of my home in Portland, Oregon, to head south for a few months. I was eventually going to be stepping into a leadership position at a church, which meant I needed to have everything together, or so I thought. That job came and went as well as working coffee shop jobs, living in a Volkswagen van, moving into a house, and eventually making San Diego, California home.

The rest of these stories are the prayers, posts, and stories scattered throughout a new season of life overriding an old one. New doesn't always mean better. Sometimes it's still hard; it's just different, which could mean it's better even when it doesn't feel that way.

Fifty Whole Cents

I'm in Portland, packing up my house and visiting friends before relocating to California. Over the weekend my friend Amanda asked whether I would visit her second-grade class and teach a writers' workshop. I was to tell a story, draw pictures, and hopefully spark some ideas for the kids to write their own stories. I love storytelling. When I figure out how to make money doing it, the world in which we live is going to look drastically different, if I may be so bold. Stories will change the world. If told well, believed fully, and birthed into action, I do believe stories will change the world. Stories are why people believe what they believe. Be it parables or cold, hard facts, stories are the who, what, when, where, why, and how of our everyday lives.

I believe in a book of stories that forever changed the way I see life, The Chronicles of Narnia. And then, of course, there's the Bible.

While my initial response to Amanda's request for me to come to her classroom and impact little minds to become good storytellers and writers was an immediate yes, my insides were a bit hesitant. I was hesitant not because I didn't want to (I really, really wanted to), but I had never done anything like that before, and I didn't know what I would do or what I would say. "Can I *read* a story?" I asked Amanda, thinking she would be quite all right with my ability to mimic the voice of any character to make any story come to life.

She laughed. "No way," she said, "you are such a good storyteller. You have to tell one of your own."

I was surprised since I was already practicing my favorite character. "But," I said, "I don't know what story to tell."

"You have *so* many stories," Amanda said. "Tell a story about something you have experience with."

I laughed. "Okay ... eating disorders, depression, suicidal thoughts, heartbreak. Which one do you think I should start with for second graders?"

Amanda giggled as only Amanda does. "Okay," she said, "tell a story about something they can relate to or could think about in their own lives. What about a pet?"

"My favorite dog, Biscuit, ran away when I was in college, and I cried so hard that I almost stopped breathing. I couldn't eat biscuits for a long time without getting emotional." The room of girls laughed. We were in the middle of a girls' night when Amanda first posed the question.

"What about your family?" Amanda yelled as she laughed. "The kids love to talk about their families. Tell a story about your family!"

"Sure," I said jokingly, "where should I start? Divorce, betrayal, lying, dysfunction, addiction, more heartbreak?" The room did a half-laugh. You know the one; it starts as a laugh and then ends in an "Awwwww, I'm sorry" tone. I am at the point where I can laugh about my family dysfunction, and I really did mean it as a joke, even though I also really did mean what I said about my family. And I guess while I might be able to laugh about my family stuff, most of that is because it helps me accept it, not because I am happy about the state of it.

"I don't know how to tell a story to second graders," I said, "I tell stories, but now that I think about it, most of them are depressing, and they offer hope, but the hope is there because of the depressing stuff. I can't talk to second graders about that."

We all continued to laugh, and Amanda told me not to worry

about it, that I would be great, but I was really worried about it. I knew it was "just" a second-grade class, but I don't believe in treating any opportunity as "just" an opportunity or any people as "just" people, no matter how old, young, big, or small.

I said yes to the opportunity, not at all prepared or having any idea what I was even going to talk about. Monday rolled around, and I prayed that morning as I had the night before for God to give me a story. "These are your kids," I said to Him. "What do I say? What do You want me to say?"

I was to be at the school at one o'clock that afternoon. The school is located on Sauvie Island, which is what it sounds like, an island outside of Portland. It's an island in the country where there are fields of almost every kind of fruit and flower you can think of. Before you hit the beaches, you hit stands of local farmers who are selling honey and whatever crop they are growing that season. You pass cows and tractors and trees perfect for climbing. Sauvie Island is the perfect combination of beach life and country life.

Seeing as how I get around by scooter, I figured it would take me a little longer than the average car to get to Sauvie Island, so I left around 11:45, leaving me time to get gas and sight-see for a bit. I love making time to take in my surroundings when I drive somewhere instead of just rushing to get where I am going—well, in most cases. Even on the way to the school, I still had no idea what I was going to talk about. I had no idea what story to tell, especially what story would be appropriate for second graders. I asked God as I scooted through the industrial section of Northwest Portland.

"Dude, what should I say? What do You want me to say? I know they are just second graders, but that doesn't exempt them from hearing what You might want to say to them." I know, perhaps I do take things a little too seriously. Maybe I overthink things to the point of stressing myself out to an unnecessary degree, but perhaps that's not always a bad thing. Perhaps it's because I care about who I interact with, even if they are "just" second graders.

I crossed the bridge to Sauvie Island, still with no story to tell. I was getting closer to the school. I breathed in the fresh country air and took in the colors of all the wildflowers and thanked God for the drive. "Help me not to miss where I am because I'm so focused on where I'm going," I prayed. "This is beautiful. Thank You so much for *this*." And as I took in the moment, it hit me. A childhood memory came flooding back to me, and my story began to unfold.

I was probably in the second grade when it happened, though I'd have to check the newspaper article to remember accurately. My favorite part of going to the grocery store with my mom was getting a quarter for the gumball machine on the way out. There was a row of machines outside our local grocery store with candy and stickers and little toys that easily broke. Well, before I had an eating disorder and went to the grocery store to find food to binge on, I was just a little kid who had to tag along with her mother, anxiously waiting to leave so she could use her quarter to get a gumball, sticker, or a toy that easily broke, depending on what she felt like that week. The days of the gumball machines are some of the last times I remember having a mildly healthy relationship with a grocery store.

After a rough week of having to share more than normal due to my above-average selfish tendencies, I went with my mom to the grocery store where I was awarded *two* quarters for good behavior. Instead of getting two smaller toys for a quarter a piece, I opted for the big machine, the one I thought I would never be able to afford my whole life, *the fifty-cent machine*. The fifty-cent machine had bigger and better toys. Understandably so ... they were fifty whole cents!

I put my quarters in the machine. Anxious to get the toy I never thought I would get (without even really knowing if I wanted it because you couldn't pick which toy), I stuck my hand up the machine where the toy was supposed to pop out. I reached in before I was even done turning the knob, and just as the second quarter when down, SNAP!

I'm still not exactly sure how it happened; it just happened. I went to pull my hand out of the machine, except nothing happened. I pulled, I pushed, I shook the machine; and there, as if it had always been a part of it, was my little hand stuck inside the machine. I yelled to my mom to come help me, who originally thought I was playing around, but as she tried to poke and prod and pull, she too realized I really was stuck.

I started to panic as I envisioned spending the rest of my life with my arm stuck in a gumball machine; either that or having no arm at all due to amputation (even as a kid, I was an overthinker). When my mother realized she was unable to get my hand out of the gumball machine, she found a store clerk to help. When the store clerk realized she couldn't get my hand out of the gumball machine, she went and found the store manager.

The store manager thought he was coming to the rescue with Windex as he tried to spray it up the toy portal, thinking he could make it slippery enough for my hand to just slip right out. A crowd had begun to gather around the machines outside the grocery store as grown men tried to pull a little girl loose from the death grip of a gumball machine. What was supposed to be a quick trip to the grocery store turned into a town gathering of all ages. After the store manager had no success, the fire department was called, and then the cops showed up. Leave it to me, even as a second grader, to draw a crowd, not because I had done anything special but because I was stuck in my own mess.

I was missing snack time, as well as play time, all because this gumball machine I had been once so drawn to because of what it had to offer wouldn't let me go. I was stuck, and while the attention might have been nice for a little while, I didn't want to be stuck anymore. After almost an hour, the men finally decided to take the machine apart. They couldn't break it because they didn't want to hurt me, so they gathered some tools and began taking the whole unit apart. It was a simple solution that was a last resort probably because people thought there was no way it would be that hard to get my little hand out of a gumball machine.

Piece by piece, the machine came apart; and finally, as the last part lifted, my hand popped out, and the crowd cheered. I cried tears of joy as strong men patted me on the back for being so brave. For as victorious a moment as it was, I can't help but look back at what possibly could have been the starting point for repeating a lot of negative patterns in my life.

When my hand was finally set free from the machine, it wasn't just my hand that came out. It was my hand death-gripping the toy I had been so anxious to get. In fact, one of the firemen had commented that my hand was stuck in such a way that if I had just let go of the toy while it was inside the machine, my hand would have fallen right out. It was my refusal to let go that had kept me stuck for so long. And it was my inability to share with anyone that I was refusing to let go that had prevented anyone from being able to help me.

There, surrounded by a crowd, I was alone in my struggle as I held on tightly to what I thought I wanted more than anything, all the while only lengthening the time spent stuck inside instead of living in freedom beyond the double glass doors, glass doors in great need of some Windex.

If I had just been in an open-fisted position, ready to receive the toy instead of reaching for it prematurely, or if I had just *let it go* once I realized I'd grabbed onto it too soon, I could have avoided the chaos of getting stuck and the calling in of the troops to get me unstuck. Everybody watched me flail around in my own mess, only for my selfish nature to be revealed at the end of the longer-than-necessary process ... all because I wouldn't let it go.

I started crying as I scooted past the flower fields on Sauvie Island. I started crying because for as much as I knew God had given me that story to share with the second graders, I also knew He had given me that story because the second grader in me was still alive and well, clinging to what she thought she wanted more than anything else. And all the while it kept her stuck, unable to go outside and live her own life.

I cried because I knew what it was, as a thirty-year-old, that I didn't want to let go of— a certain on-again, off-again relationship. It held greater value than the gumball machine toy did, and that made it even harder to let go. Just as I had that day in the grocery store, crying because I was stuck due to my own death grip, I cried as I thought about how stuck I currently felt, prolonging a process simply because I don't want to let it go, all in fear because I might not get what I wanted.

I dried my tears and joined the second graders at Sauvie Island Elementary School. I added animation and dramatization, and I made the story as lively as possible while talking about the importance of sharing, being willing to wait, and letting go when you need to. I knew I was talking to myself as much as I was to those second graders. I told them about the power of story and that even as a thirty-year-old, I was still learning from my own stories when I was their age. I told them I was still learning to let go and that it was still hard, even as an adult. "Write your stories down," I said to them. "Write down everything that happens to you. Your stories will help a lot of people."

Little hands shot up as they asked questions and shared some of their own stories. When I asked them the moral of the story I had shared with them, I called on a little girl in the front, who wiggled her hand in the air. She put her finger to her mouth and thought for a second. "Well," she said, "just be patient."

My face smiled as my heart felt hope. Yes, it was "just" a little girl in the second grade responding to a question, but it sounded more like God's response to me as I have asked Him time and time again about this one thing I think I want more than anything, unsure of my ability to let it go and trust Him with it.

"Just be patient," He says to me, and the sound of His voice is not limited to that of a grown man or woman's, the rolling of a thunderstorm, the blazing of a fire, or the crashing of a wave. All too often I ask God to reveal Himself to me in signs and wonders, to speak louder and clearer, and to unleash His great love for me in a mighty way. And sometimes He does. But most times, He doesn't. He tries to catch my attention in the smallest of details I miss every day, all because I am too busy looking for the biggest and the best, assuming that bigger is better and louder is clearer.

But yesterday afternoon, on a carpet covered with second graders, God whispered to me through the voice of a little girl with kinky brunette hair. "Just be patient," she said, and God gave me a vision of my second-grade self, with my own kinky brunette hair, letting go of that toy and skipping outside to live my life. When I envisioned it, I couldn't see whether the toy was in my hand or not when I walked outside. I don't know whether in letting it go I got the toy back or whether I never got it at all. All I know is, it doesn't matter. I was perfectly content being outside in the sun instead of stuck behind glass in need of Windex, death-gripped to a machine full of things that easily break.

It felt like a fresh start in my thirties to live a life in which history doesn't have to repeat itself. I wrote about my adult version of the gumball machine toy this morning, and as best as I knew how, I let it go. It's time for me to get myself unstuck and trust my God when He says, "Just be patient."

"Growth is painful. Change is painful. But nothing is as painful as staying stuck somewhere you don't belong," as someone said on Pinterest.

Thank you, Ms. Amanda, for letting me share my fifty-whole-cents with your second graders. It did an unexpected amount of healing for the second grader in me.

Confessions of a Youth Leader

It was a beautiful day on Saturday, but what day isn't beautiful in San Diego? Coming from an extended dark spell in Portland, I wanted to get outside and enjoy the day, but since I was asked to speak on Sunday morning, I decided to confine myself to my friend's apartment and work on my talk. It was a nice enough idea, but instead of working on my talk, I Skyped with my friends in Portland, wasted time on Facebook, and proceeded to stress myself out over the talk.

I felt like I needed to make up for the time I had wasted on social media by watching a Tim Keller sermon on YouTube almost as a form of punishment. I love Tim Keller, so it's not that I thought listening to him was a form of punishment, I guess I felt like I needed to make up for my wasted time by learning something or doing something "godly" so He wouldn't be mad at me and make my talk go horrible—He being God. And yes, I am embarrassed to admit that I actually have that poor of a view of God—the God I'm supposed to be representing, not just as a leader in a church but as a Christian in how I live my everyday life. I live like He is waiting to smite me. How many spades must one's life reveal? As many as it takes, I suppose.

But I couldn't focus on anything Tim Keller was saying, and it felt even more wasteful to zone out to Tim Keller than it did to get caught up in social media or at the very least do something I enjoy; so I made guacamole and turned on *Parks and Recreation*. Surely goodness, God would agree that there's always time for *Parks and Recreation*, and one-liners from Ron Swanson are a necessity, especially during times of high stress.

After *Parks and Recreation*, I still felt bad. I confined myself to stay home on a nice day to work on my talk, and not only was I missing the nice day, but I was avoiding working on my talk. I had nothing to show for my time spent inside except making myself feel lazy and crazy the longer I avoided it. I stressed out, so naturally I looked for chocolate.

This is how some youth leaders prepare for a message on Sunday, at least this one, who is honest about the state of her humanity. My need for divine intervention keeps me not only humble but also employed.

This could make for an interesting job.

Puffy Yellow Jackets

I have to speak at a high school this week, and I have to be honest (go figure), I don't want to. I don't want to because sometimes I wonder whether it even all matters. I don't want to because while I know how to hold my ground, sometimes kids are just mean, not even to me but to each other. I recently heard a friend say, "Politeness costs nothing," and I couldn't agree more. But how do you get a kid to believe in being kind and polite, especially when they think their reputation is on the line? The only thing that comes up is a story from my youth and a hope that it translates to kids of all ages.

I remember being in the seventh grade and someone pointing out a Roxy surfer girl model in a *Seventeen* magazine. A girl in our friend group pointed her out and said, "JJ, this looks like you when you get older." The girl she pointed at was a short-haired brunette who was clearly a tomboy. She didn't look like the other models, but she was still a model, and she was cute in a tomboy kind of way. It was the first compliment I remember getting as a middle schooler. Like most middle schoolers, I was awkward and underdeveloped but without the obvious potential other girls had to be high school heartthrobs.

For example, I didn't make the cheerleading team, so I borrowed a cheerleading uniform from a girl who did, and I had my mom take cheerleading photos in our front yard. Not only were they unattractive, there was a mud pit behind me.

I was approached by boys but only to talk to my friends for them. I never understood why boys didn't like me. But in seventh grade I got my first compliment regarding my looks or my potential looks—one day, just maybe one day, way after high school, I might look like a 1990s tomboy model.

I was excited by the thought and wondered how long I would have to wait. One of the boys who overheard the comment being made about my future self walked over and asked whether he could see the picture. "Wow, yeah, I could see that," he said, and my excitement grew ... until he kept talking. "If that's true, call me then but not before."

Excitement dwindled, and the reality of my present self came crashing down on my two-minute-long dream of becoming a 1990s tomboy model. Everyone laughed, so naturally I laughed too, because that's what you do when you're in middle school and you don't want to let on that you've been hurt. Except that it's not what you *should* do. Never on your behalf or the behalf of others should you silence your voice and laugh with the crowd for the sake of fitting in. But in middle school I didn't understand that, and truth be told, sometimes I still forget, because it feels good to fit in, even when it hurts.

By the time I reached ninth grade, my five-year relationship with braces ended. I remember the day I got them off. I couldn't stop licking my teeth; they felt so slimy and perfect. It was the first time something on me ever felt perfect. I went to youth group that night, and a boy pointed out that I had gotten my braces off. Everyone was outside, scattered on the field in front of the church for a game of dodgeball. Huffing and puffing while trying to dodge a big, red rubber ball, a boy ran up to me. "You ... you ... you got your braces off!" he said, followed by deep breaths.

"Yeah." I smiled, not moving so as not to mess up my smile or get slime on my mouth.

"It looks good," he said, followed by the loud smack of him being hit in the head with a big, red rubber ball.

"You're out!" a kid yelled, and I wanted to attack that kid for interrupting my first compliment from a boy.

I said thank you to the boy as he walked off the field. "Are you cold?" he asked as he started to take off his puffy yellow jacket and walk back toward me.

I lied and said, "A little bit," given the slightest possibility that a boy might offer me his jacket.

"GET OFF THE FIELD. YOU'RE OUT" the kid yelled again at the boy with the puffy yellow jacket, who liked my slimy smile.

"HE IS!" I turned and yelled. "HE'S GIVING ME HIS JACKET! I'M COLD!" I lied with confidence and a death stare that shut that kid right up. Don't mess with an awkward girl on the outskirts of middle school when she is getting her first compliment from a boy.

He handed me his jacket, and I took it, still uncertain why he had offered it but pretty sure it was because of my teeth. I went home that night and wrote a thank-you card to my orthodontist. Seriously. I have believed in thank-you cards for as long as I can remember. Once again, thank you Dr. Ross Orthodontics. I still get compliments on my teeth, and I can't exactly take the credit.

All this to say to my present self (because I'm forgetful) and anyone willing to listen, especially in middle and high school, "Be nice to people." While we all strive so hard to do something great and be somebody worth remembering, sometimes being someone worth remembering is as simple as just being nice.

With love as the lenses you look through, speak truth to people about who they will become but also speak truth to them about who they are now. Tell people they don't have to wait to be great one day. Tell them they are great now, growing into someone greater. Life is hard, and middle school is harder. High school follows, and it doesn't exactly get easier. Kids need to be told they are smart, funny, beautiful, brilliant, and fully capable of thinking for themselves and voicing their truths.

Kids grow up, all of them, even the awkward ones, and they remember. They remember who picked on them, and they remember who was nice to them. They remember the boy who wanted the girl to call him one day if she grew up pretty, and they remember the boy who risked getting smacked in the head by a big, red rubber ball so he could tell a girl he liked her smile. Nine times out of ten, the girl never calls the first boy, but I guarantee you, no matter how old she gets, she still smiles and licks her slimy teeth when she sees puffy yellow jackets.

Somebody Poisoned the Water Bottle

I was going to have a productive day yesterday; at least that was the plan. But then I drank bleach, and that has a tendency to put a damper on your plans.

I hadn't considered this until the bleach was in my system, sucking the air right out of me as I lay nearly prostrate on the floor, trying to get the bleach up and out of my mouth. I was surrounded by people who were trying to figure out what was wrong with me. Assuming I was choking, a man began to give me the Heimlich maneuver. I proceeded to vomit up my smoothie from earlier in the morning, but to no avail was I able to catch my breath. I tried to point at the Nalgene water bottle sitting on the counter and managed to croak out something to the effect of "Something's in there."

My coworker looked at the bottle and instantly knew I wasn't choking. "She's not choking," he said in a very calm and monotone manner. "She drank bleach." He knew I had drunk bleach because *he* was the one who had put the bleach in my water bottle and left it sitting on the counter.

By now you may have realized I didn't intentionally drink bleach to put a damper on my plans for a productive day. I *accidentally* drank bleach to put a damper on my plans for a productive day. What you may not yet realize is the fact that my coworker didn't intentionally bleach my water bottle either. And so the story goes ...

I have a Nalgene water bottle. Mostly I drink from it at home because it's a great way to keep track of how much water I'm drinking. With the heat consistently rising in San Diego, water consumption has become even more important, at least to me and my proneness to severe dehydration. I had noticed over the last few days that I couldn't find my water bottle, but I didn't think too much about it, assuming it would show up at some point in time.

In the meantime my coworker and good friend who had been borrowing my van found a Nalgene water bottle. Unsure of what person might have left it in the van, never having seen me drink from it before, and under the assumption of "finder's keepers," he decided to clean the water bottle so he might become its new owner. He took his newfound water bottle with him to work, put a little bleach in the bottom, and filled the rest with water, leaving it to sit for a while to clear out all the germs. And by a while I mean overnight.

Enter me, coming in to open the coffee shop the following morning, surprised and excited to find my water bottle. Unsure of how it got there, I knew it would be only a matter of time before my water bottle turned up again, so I didn't question it. It was even full of water, I thought. "Awesome." I had yet to discover how not awesome it was. I proceeded with the morning tasks of opening the shop. It was nearly 90 degrees inside and only six o'clock in the morning.

Shortly after my manager arrived and only an hour into the work day, with machines pumping out heat, no air-conditioning, and the rising temperature inside the small space where we made coffee, an executive decision was made to shut down the shop for the sake of the employees' well-being. My manager and I were soaking through our clothes by seven o'clock. As we regrettably turned customers away but gratefully prepared for our exit out of the hot box we felt trapped in, I gathered my things and put ice into my already-filled water bottle.

I assured my manager that I thought she had made the right

decision to close and that I was extremely grateful. "Someone is going to complain no matter what," I said. "If it's not the customers, it's the employees. Honestly, I think it's a good thing for the employees to feel cared for." She thanked me for the assurance. We laughed about how damp our clothes were and proceeded to pack up. Just before putting on my backpack, I grabbed my water bottle. Eager to get some water in my system, and without the slightest clue as to what was about to happen, I took a big gulp.

As soon as the water hit the inside of my mouth, I knew something was wrong. I swallowed the littlest bit before trying with all my might to spit it out of my mouth. My whole mouth and throat felt like it went numb as if I had no control, and it slowly felt like everything was closing up and I couldn't breathe. I was making noises as if I were choking because I couldn't breathe. I didn't know what was happening.

My manager began to yell that I was choking. I didn't think I was choking, but I couldn't say anything. I couldn't talk, I couldn't yell, I couldn't breathe. I was gasping for air in a confusing amount of pain. Everything was burning, and I couldn't quite communicate that something was in the water I had drunk.

There is a FedEx business center right next to my coffee shop, and a lifeguard who fortunately needed to mail something that day ran over immediately. He began asking me questions, but I couldn't get enough air to talk. He proceeded to give me the Heimlich maneuver, trying to make me throw up, which I did little by little, unsure whether it was helping. I finally pointed to the water bottle. By that time my coworker who had bleached the water bottle in the first place had come by the shop to get coffee and ran over when my manager yelled that I was choking. Little did I know when I pointed to the water bottle that he knew what had happened. I can't imagine what he must have been feeling in that moment, but I can imagine it probably didn't feel very good.

Amid all the chaos and my kneeling on the floor and continuing to try to catch my breath while spitting up what I could, the message was finally received that I had swallowed bleach. The lifeguard quickly stopped doing the Heimlich, told someone to look up poison control, and called the paramedics as he rubbed my back and told me to breathe. He asked my manager my name and coached me through the process. "You're doing good, JJ. You're doing good. Just breathe."

Something about the way he talked to me was helpful; it kept me living in the moment instead of slipping into panic. Though the lifeguard didn't know me, hearing my name called made me feel like it mattered if something happened to me or not. It was personal. I was a person, not just a victim. I didn't get to thank the lifeguard, but I was so thankful he had been there. I was so thankful for the person or reason he needed to go to FedEx that day.

I've been in a traumatic situation before, in which I knew allowing panic or worry to set in would only make it worse, at least for your breathing. I knew the importance of needing to stay in the moment, even if the moment felt awful or scary.

My first thought upon swallowing the bleach and realizing what was happening was, *I'm not going to die, but this is not going to be good.* I tried to do what I could to remain present. Although I couldn't speak, in my mind I took note of everything. *I can feel the man's hand on my back. My hands are touching the floor. The floor is pretty dirty. I think it needs to be swept. I can see everyone's feet. Someone is not wearing shoes.* Unable to breathe but knowing panic would make it worse, I kept present as best as I knew how, focusing neither on what I had done or what might happen to me, but I chose to be in the moment, even if the moment involved lying on a cold, dirty floor at the feet of people around me. The moment felt awful and scary but knowing I was in it kept me alert, which kept me barely breathing.

There was one instance in which I found it nearly impossible to catch my breath, and a bit more fear crept in to the point of having to check in with my Creator. *God,* I said in my heart and mind, *I'm not going to die, right? This isn't how I go. This can't be how I go.* Being able to talk to God while unable to talk to those around me helped me feel not so alone in the pain, and I knew He wouldn't let me go that way.

Reassured that I wasn't going to die, I regained my focus. The paramedics showed up, and I tried to communicate that I didn't want to go in the ambulance, but they insisted that I do. Unable to do much arguing or even breathing, I figured I better listen.

I could hear them all talking around me, asking questions about what had happened and how it had happened. Was it intentional? Was it an accident? Who had put bleach in my water bottle and why? I heard my friend trying to explain it. He still didn't know it was my water bottle; he thought I'd drunk from the one he'd found, unsure as to why I would do that. Fair enough.

I was loaded into the ambulance, accompanied by a paramedic intern by the name of Kevin. My breathing began to normalize. Kevin was kind and kept me smiling and laughing, which is a sure sign I am doing okay. "I wanted to be in air-conditioning today," I said to Kevin in a whisper since it was difficult to talk.

"Well, it looks like you're gonna get that," he said.

"Yeah, and I like to be driven around, kind of like Ms. Daisy." I wondered whether he would know which movie I referred to.

"This is kind of an expensive way to get driven around," Kevin said.

I laughed. "Come on, man, I'm trying to look on the bright side here."

Kevin laughed and apologized. When he and the other paramedic found out I was from the south, they asked whether I could turn on a southern accent. I told them I could; I did, and they laughed.

"Thank y'all so much," I said as they pulled me out of the ambulance. They laughed at me saying "y'all" and said they liked it. "Bless yer little hearts," I responded. And while I was joking, I meant it, too, not in a condescending way but in a *Lord, really bless them* kind of way.

Once inside the hospital, I was hooked up to machines while nurses took vitals. I couldn't help but have feelings of déjà vu. Would I ever get out of hospital debt? "This is JJ," the paramedics introduced me. "She accidentally drank bleach."

I couldn't help but laugh a little. It all sounded so ridiculous, even to the nurses who looked at me and then back at the paramedics. "Accidentally? Are you sure?" they asked.

"Definitely an accident," one of the paramedics responded, and I felt known. The nurses asked whether someone had put bleach in my water bottle on purpose. Had someone been trying to play a joke on me? I said it was definitely an accident on both accounts.

"Are you sure you drank it accidentally?" the nurse asked me.

"I'm sure," I said.

"So you're not suicidal?" she asked due to protocol.

"I'm not," I whispered. "I'm really hot and tired, but I'm not suicidal."

She didn't laugh. "Have you ever been suicidal?" she asked.

That was a loaded question and one I didn't want to unload in that moment given how difficult it was to carry on a conversation due to the burning sensation in my throat. I smiled and said no. I can admit that there was a time and place in my life when I would have wished that bleach would have been my end, but this wasn't that time or place; and that was enough for me to be grateful and leave that pain in the past.

After the nurse left, a doctor came in to see me. He was probably really good at being a doctor, but he wasn't as good at bedside manner. As my aunt would say, "He didn't even have curbside manner!" After being short and factual with me, he said there wasn't much they could do past monitoring me for a little while to make sure the bleach didn't get into the rest of my system.

"A little household bleach isn't going to kill you," he said without laughing or implying he was trying to make me feel better. I thought about this experienced doctor, and I thought about Kevin, the intern; and while their titles might imply that one knew more than the other or had a higher status, it was the intern, not the doctor, who made me feel better. It was the intern who actually made me feel like I was going to be okay. Like the lifeguard who called me by name, Kevin treated me like a person. The doctor treated me like a patient, a bed number, a "girl in room twenty-two."

I think when people are treated as people, they realize they matter, and hope is heightened, even restored. While certain issues may need to be addressed physically or emotionally, having hope to live or make it through a certain situation is just the grit some people need to strive toward getting those issues addressed. Laughing with Kevin made me feel alive and gave me grit to follow instructions to take care of myself. Those instructions mattered, and so did I.

After lying in the hospital bed for a while, my friends showed up, both my manager and the coworker who had put bleach in the water bottle. He was even kind enough to bring the water bottle with him and asked whether I was thirsty, followed by "Too soon?" He asked why I would drink from his water bottle, and I told him it wasn't his water bottle; it was mine. He disagreed with me and said he'd found it and had been bleaching it to clean it. "You found it because I lost it! The top of that water bottle says 'faith,' and you're telling me that's your water bottle?" I asked, knowing he would never write "faith" on anything he owned.

He looked at the top of the water bottle and read the word *faith*. His eyes got big. "Oh I'm so sorry," he said, followed by a few apologetic swear words.

My friends sat by me while we watched reruns of *The Fresh Prince of Bel-Air* and drank almond milk. I was glad not to be alone. I was given something to numb my throat, and it lasted for about fifteen minutes before the burning sensation returned. A new doctor came to see me and was much kinder than the previous one. He made eye contact and smiled; he talked calmly to me with care in his voice. I hadn't realized until that moment that it had been such a long time since I had been talked to like that. I took note of his wedding ring and the fact that his name tag revealed his name to be the same as my ex-boyfriend.

I laughed to myself because of all the silly places my mind goes. *He's a doctor doing his job, JJ,* I reassured myself. *Let him be good at his job without it meaning anything and let him have the same name as your ex without it being a sign. It's not a sign.* The doctor told me I couldn't eat anything hard or salty for the next couple of days. "Like chips," he said. My friend laughed because he knew chips and guacamole were without a doubt my favorite food group.

After three hours, I was dismissed from the hospital. "I'm sorry I put bleach in your water bottle," my friend said, and he took me to get a peanut butter smoothie. "Do you hate me?" he asked.

"Why would I hate you?" I asked back.

"Because I put bleach in your water bottle and almost killed you."

"You didn't do it on purpose, and no, I don't hate you."

But almost every hour he checked back in. "Do you hate me? I'm sorry I bleached your water bottle." I told him he was already forgiven and that he didn't need to keep apologizing ... but he did.

"You are forgiven," I said. "Let that absorb."

I thought about all this as I woke up this morning with less of a burning sensation in my throat. I thought about how sometimes we do things we don't mean to do, and people get hurt in the process. I thought about how disappointed God must be in me sometimes for consistently getting so much so wrong. I thought about how often I say sorry and how rarely I hear that I'm forgiven, not because forgiveness is being withheld but because I can't hear it over my guilt and shame. It feels better to work toward my forgiveness, to either consistently apologize or do something to make up for it. But God isn't asking me to do either of those things, and He's usually never as disappointed as I assume Him to be. God is constantly asking me to absorb the forgiveness, to neither focus on what I did do nor to worry about what will happen but to live in the moment of being forgiven, no matter how uncomfortable it may be.

I'm starting over today, or at least I'm trying to. For the last few to six months, I've been functioning as a girl who has forgotten who she is and how God sees her—as a person, not a victim, who matters and is loved beyond belief. When you function out of such forgetfulness, it makes it hard to see other people as people who matter and are loved beyond belief too, which makes it easy to become selfish without even realizing it. I think it's my selfishness that sometimes sickens me the most, a truth much harder to swallow than bleach. I am incredibly selfish.

One doesn't need to drink bleach in order to make themself sick; one just needs to try to be their own god for a while. A good God has the best interest of everyone at hand, literally *everyone*. I'm not a good God.

The day before I drank the bleach, I was talking to my best friend, Anna, on the phone. I was telling her how I had been lately, most of which involved being incredibly drained and weary on top of feeling like a complete and utter disappointment. "Bud," Anna said, "it sounds like you've lost touch with God's heart for you, and that's an exhausting place to be." We talked through my disconnect and about how much I didn't want to be in a desperate place again.

"It's gonna hurt to feel desperate again," Anna said, "but at least you'll have breath in your lungs." I wrote down what she had said, and I tried not to pout.

As I lay in the hospital bed the morning after that conversation, I thanked God for breath in my lungs, the very breath I'd had a hard time catching just a few hours prior. "I'm desperate, God," I whispered.

I said it then, and I say it again now. I'm desperate for something greater than myself. Aren't we all? I'm desperate for God.

And in that desperation, I'm finding it just a little bit easier to breathe again.

Just a Rose

At thirteen years old, I fell in love with the high school quarterback. Not only did I fall in love with him, but everybody in my middle and high school knew I had fallen in love with him. At the time the middle and high school shared the same building with separate hallways, and as an eighth grader, the high school side of the hallway seemed sacred. It was sacred not because it was a rite of passage or an unknown world of what it meant to be cool and old (in a young way); it was sacred because Jordan Pate walked those hallways.

It's fair to say that as a thirteen-year-old, I was obsessed. I was also awkward and not aesthetically pleasing to the eye, but it didn't matter much to me because I was obsessed.

I called it love, but as I look back on the fact that I bought pictures of Jordan from his sister for two dollars apiece (mind you, I had a stack) and even went so far as to blow up his football picture and turn it into a poster, I think it's safe to say that Jordan Pate was my Justin Beiber, which is to say what I already said— I was obsessed. I know it sounds crazy, and in some ways it was, but in the same way that a lot of girls have posters of their favorite boy bands and the famous guys they think they love, so was I with a guy who went to my high school.

While a lot of my friends went to the football games to see or be seen by other people, I remember wanting to be death-gripped to the chain-link fence the entire time, watching Jordan flawlessly dominate the game. After he graduated, I mourned and eventually found a healthier obsession of being in love with complete strangers, the Hanson brothers.

I loved watching Jordan on the football field; it was like he owned it, and I was in awe. I think anytime you watch someone do what they were created to do or function in a way that makes them feel alive, it draws you in, and you can't help but watch. Maybe the guys wanted to be Jordan, and the girls wanted to be with him, or vice versa (who knows anymore), but there was something about watching him function as a football player that made you want whatever it was he had.

I think competition has the potential to bring out the best in people because it drives them to do better, perform better, live better. I also think competition has the potential to bring out the worst in people when the sole focus of one's life becomes comparing oneself to others, edging people out, and always trying to get ahead of the game without a care in the world for who's in it.

During my eighth-grade year, I had a science teacher who happened to be Jordan's football coach, and it didn't take long for him to discover the fan girl in me. On Valentine's Day way back in the 1990s before the Hanson brothers, there was a knock on the door of the science lab, to which my teacher responded, "I think we have a surprise visitor." When the door opened, it was as if the clouds parted, the lights from heaven shone forth, and the angels sang as Jordan Pate came walking through the door. My jaw dropped, and I froze as he made his way over to my lab table.

He smiled as he approached me, extended a rose, and said something to the effect of, "Happy Valentine's Day. I got this for you." I was pretty sure my ears popped and my whole body stopped functioning, as if I had blacked out and wasn't sure what was happening. I sat deadpan in my chair, unable to breathe, as I tried to say, "Thank you," but all I could get out was a gasp. I couldn't even reach for the rose. I just stared at him. Eventually he set the rose on my table since I wasn't budging, and I watched him as he walked back out, the whole class cheering and chanting and patting me on the back.

Like with everyone, I grew up, and so did he; and our paths never really crossed again. There was no agenda with him being kind to me in that way. He got nothing out of it other than giving a young girl the best day of her life up to that point. It was just a rose from a gas station, but it remains a memory that will never be forgotten ... a ninety-nine-cent memory (it was the nineties, and roses were cheaper). His kindness changed the way I saw him, even on the football field. I was in awe of his talent but more so by his ability not to get so caught up in his talent that he failed to notice the people on the sidelines, cheering him on.

I love a good competition and watching people try so hard to be the best they can be in their attempt to dominate in their sport. But more so than being the best they can be on the field, I love when people try to be the best they can be off the field, perhaps when other people aren't looking. I love when people are kind to people, even when it's of no advantage to them. I love when the rough-and-tough football player takes that little extra time before school to buy a rose and give it to the little eighth grader who never really felt noticed by anyone.

That's what I call winning at life.

Betsy Betsys

When I first met Betsy, she was naked. I know it sounds weird, but that's how the women's locker room goes at the YMCA. Naked is normal. As I approached my locker, I tried to shimmy past her as un-awkwardly as possible, but she was naked, and I was not; so despite my attempts to act normal, I think I came across as nervous and clumsy, dropping my shoes and shampoo bottle. Betsy was unphased by my awkwardness, and I liked this about her.

"How was your workout?" she asked in a chipper tone.

"Oh," I said, somewhat caught off guard, "you know" (even though she didn't). "It was ... well ... I got my butt kicked," I said honestly. And I did.

"Don't you just love those days?" Betsy asked. "Of course, not while you're getting your butt kicked," she said as she lathered lotion all over her body, "but after you finish, you feel so much better. What's your workout?"

"Spinning," I said. "Well, I'm just getting back into it."

"Are you new to the Y?"

"Well, I started coming over the summer, but I've been back and forth between here and Portland, so ... kind of yes and no."

Her eyes lit up when I said Portland, and she said she loved the Pacific Northwest. I liked her even more.

We talked about Portland for a while as she put clothes on, and I awkwardly tried to take clothes off before hopping in the shower. She told me about her daughter, who went to school in Portland, and her husband, who had died five years ago. She told me she was still in the grieving process, and I thought that was beautiful and sad but mostly beautiful. I thought it was beautiful because as she talked about the struggle of the grieving process and having to pull herself out of bed sometimes, it was reflective of the fact that she lived well and had loved someone hard—so hard that five years down the road, she still missed him.

I told her I agreed with her about hating the butt-kicking process of working out but loving the effect it had on the mind and body afterward. I told her I was depression prone and that I had gotten to the point in my life that I decided I was going to have to start making choices for my well-being regardless of how I felt. "There are times I don't feel like getting out of bed," I told her, "but I choose to. Same with working out. I hate going to that spinning class, but I go because I love how I feel afterward."

Betsy smiled and said she couldn't agree more. "My husband was a depressive," she said. "There were days I had to say, 'Get your butt up cause that might be the only thing that helps!'" I thought that to be a good point.

People don't often know how to help people with depression. And I get it; there doesn't seem to be much to do to help, but I know what doesn't help—doing nothing. Doing nothing only makes us (the depressives) sadder, worthless feeling even; and the sadder we are, the more we want to do nothing, and so the cycle goes.

"Yeah, it's made a difference," I said to Betsy, "making choices regardless of how I feel ... I notice that my feelings are slowly catching up to my choices, to the point that now I want to go out and do things, even exercise when I know it will kick my butt." I explained that while I didn't want to get my butt kicked, I wanted to change, I wanted to get stronger, and that required a process that was hard. That I hated, but I was embracing it, not because I liked it but because it was worth it.

Betsy agreed and told me she had days, even as a teacher, when she didn't feel like getting up and teaching, but she always ended up feeling better afterward. I asked her what she taught, and she said, "Water aerobics every Monday and Wednesday morning."

I told her I had been wanting to try water aerobics, and she invited me to join her class anytime. "I'll warn you, though," she said. "I got a bunch of talkers in my class. Maybe they don't talk enough at home (I don't know), but it's hard to keep them focused." I laughed and told her I would give it a try at some point.

We talked about gluten-free food and green smoothies and the effects nutrition had on the mind and body. "It's not rocket science," Betsy said, "but it is hard." After her husband died, she didn't take very good care of herself, mostly because it was hard to care, understandably so. I can't imagine. I can't imagine having a best friend for thirty, forty-plus years, someone you made a life with, not just in the form of a home but in a kid, an actual human life made up of each of you, breathing the life you gave them. And then one day just like that, your best friend is gone. I'd lay in bed too and probably not eat well, if I ate at all.

But there was Betsy, fully clothed at this point, standing tall at about five four (I guess) with long blonde and gray hair and beautifully aged skin. Her skin evidenced she had lived a long life, but it was so smooth you'd never be able to guess how long she'd been living life with not a single dab of makeup on her face. "I may not look like I used to," Betsy said. "My skin's not as tight, but I eat well, and I exercise. And I tell ya, I've never felt better. I've decided that's what matters, how I feel. I exercise to feel good, not to look better. I'm past that." She might have thought she was past looking good, but I thought she was beautiful.

She asked about my tattoos, and I gave a brief explanation of each. She said how much she loved them and that she wanted to get one on her shoulder blade of a shooting star when she worked up enough courage. I told her I knew a place when she was ready. And that was when she extended her hand to shake mine.

"I'm Betsy," she said as she smiled.

"That's my sister's name!" I said excitedly.

"Really? Is she an Elizabeth Betsy, or a Betsy Betsy like me?"

"She's a Betsy Betsy," I said, "and I'm a JJ!"

"Betsy Betsys are rare," she said, "but so are JJs."

And there we were … two rare breeds from different walks of life, both trying to do the best we could with what we had, making choices to take care of ourselves in the midst of what life had thrown at us. I can't claim to know what it's like to lose a spouse. I could never say, "I understand," because I don't, at least not to that depth. But I do know what it's like to experience a heartbreak so deep that it makes some days hard to breathe. While perspective is always a good thing to have, your pain should never be compared to someone else's pain. Pain is pain is pain is pain. Your pain is legit, as is Betsy's, as is mine. What is painful to me isn't any less painful just because I haven't experienced the same kind of pain as Betsy.

Instead of telling myself to "suck it up" when Betsy shared her pain, I took notes on how to handle pain. I allowed myself the freedom of feeling my own pain while listening to the insight of someone who had gone through something tragic.

Since then I have been making choices, day after day after day, to take care of my mind, my body, and my heart. And day after day those choices have been adding up to make me a better me, a healthier me, a me who is more and more okay with being me. Being okay with being me is sometimes one of the most difficult things for me to do … or be. And I think I've realized that not being okay with being me is one of the most heartbreaking things for God to experience. I think this is true for all of us. Not being okay with being ourselves is what leads us to act in ways that tear down or hurt others in our self-seeking attempts to feel better about ourselves. And it's in these attempts that not only are others hurt, but we get further and further away from who we were created to be and by default further and further away from God.

The biggest part of my efforts to make choices regardless of how I feel has been the choice to believe God is who He says He is, even when it feels like He isn't. I have started to live based on the fact that *He is able*. I may have realized this before, but (1) I forget all the time, and (2) there is a difference between realizing the truth about God and living like you believe the truth about God. Regardless of what God does or doesn't do, *He is able to do anything and everything*. And *living* like I believe this has made all the difference. He is able to mend my broken heart, even if it doesn't feel mended right now; it doesn't mean I'm not on the mend. And even if I never felt mended, this doesn't change the fact that God is still able to do it. Because God is always able, there is always hope. God's ability is what gives me hope, no matter what my circumstance.

Betsy and I are both single for different reasons. I'm on the before side of marrying your best friend, and she's on the after side. While our storms may be different, our hearts are both weathered and worn, making our vessels, our bodies, a little shaky and uncertain of what lies ahead. But it's with weathered and worn hearts and shaky bodies that we move forward, full steam ahead, refusing to let our feelings or circumstances dictate our quality of life.

This morning I went to Betsy's water aerobics class. I was the youngest participant by at least thirty years and the only one without sunglasses and a hat. The sun beamed down on about twelve of us as we kicked and punched through the water, the ladies all telling me to be sure to bring a hat next time. The Beatles were blaring in the background, and I was happy.

I didn't accomplish anything great or get the accolades I sometimes think I deserve. I didn't get the phone call I wanted or the offer of a new relationship. I didn't go on another epic road trip or get the book deal I've always hoped for. I didn't get any of those things people tell you will make you happy. I stopped waiting for those things to happen, and I got up.

I got up early and jumped in a pool with a floatation device strapped to my back. Then I tried to keep up with some senior citizens as we danced and jogged and swam to the Beatles on a warm October morning in San Diego. And I was so very happy—without the accolades, without the phone call, without the relationship or the book deal.

I took a lesson from Betsy, not just in water aerobics, but in life.

I lived.

And then I thanked God … for life, the Beatles, and those rare Betsy Betsys, who bring out the rarely felt joyful JJ in me.

A Single Blade of Grass

The day didn't start as I thought it would. Unlike most days, I had a plan. The plan involved a lot of being joyful and looking on the bright side as well as working on my book and doing a lot of prayer to actually make it a reality. As soon as my feet touched down from the guest bed I'd slept in last night, I pictured the enemy saying, "Oh no, she's up." I thanked God that I had four walls to sleep behind, a bathroom to use in the morning, and most importantly, warm socks. Never underestimate the power of warm socks—a good pair can warm the heart as much as the feet.

I slid through the kitchen of my friend's house; she was out of town, so I had a four- bedroom house all to myself. After living in my Volkswagen van the last few months, it was a nice change of pace—an upgrade, if you will. I lit a Christmas candle, played Christmas music (yep, I'm one of those), and made coffee. I thanked God for all three of those things and for the month of November. I sat down to write, and I did what one should never do when he or she actually wants to focus. I checked Facebook.

I won't lie. I love seeing the little red notifications telling me I have messages or comments or likes. I like likes. Who doesn't? Before I click on my messages, I always try to guess who they might be from.

I think my love for a good guessing game stems back to the days of *Mister Rogers' Neighborhood*, when my siblings and I would guess what color sweater Mister Rogers was going to put on that day. I love the anticipation before finding out who the message is from. You still have hope it's from that certain someone, even though you tell yourself it's not. Then you wonder whether it's your sister asking for her sweater you were wearing in a picture you posted.

I wasn't ready to get the message I received yesterday. It wasn't in my realm of guessing, not even in my worst-case scenario realm, and those are pretty bad. For as much as I love those little red notifications, I knew as soon as I clicked it that I didn't want to see the one I saw yesterday.

Seeing as Facebook was the only place where I could be reached by the person who messaged me, it was Facebook that informed me an old friend had just committed suicide. I've been trying to find a gentler way to say it, but there is no gentle way to say it. I've been thinking about how I could make it less abrupt, but suicide *is* abrupt.

I felt my stomach flip inside me. I grabbed the countertop and tried to catch my breath. Thoughts, memories, hows, whys, what-ifs all raced through my head. My heart started cracking despite my refusal to accept it. None of it made sense. The news didn't make sense. How I felt about the news didn't make sense; not even life itself made sense in that moment. "I don't get it!" I yelled as I started to cry. For as much as I wanted to yell at God, I also wanted Him to hold me ... and He did. He held me while I yelled at Him. God is not an either/or God— He can hold you and you can yell at him at the same time.

I didn't know what to do with myself. I didn't know what to do with what I now knew. I wasn't prepared to wake up to that. I felt like I had just walked into battle without any armor or weapons, and I didn't know how to fight. There were so many emotions present that I didn't know what to do with them or even how to feel them all. I knew my options. I knew I could take an "I deserve this" approach to numb out the emotions, but I knew that wouldn't actually help. I crossed off my go-to unhealthy coping mechanisms as not being an option, and instead I looked up snow boots on Amazon—because that makes sense, seeing as how I live in San Diego.

I looked up snow boots because it gave me something to do, something else to focus on, because it shifted my thoughts from "This hurts" to "I need this." And in needing something tangible like snow boots, I didn't need to face the reality of loss being painful. I looked up snow boots because not even I, the girl who prides herself on living simply, am above trying to buy my way out of feeling bad. My head tells me, *You can't buy your way to happiness.* I know this from experience all too well, and yet even still, if caught off guard in just the right way, I turn right back to the lie and welcome it as truth. What's worse is that the lie is obvious to everyone; no one in their right mind would say, "Snow boots will make this all better!" And yet there I sat, scrolling through Amazon and getting angry at sellers for not having my size, when really I was angry because I was avoiding the painful truth that nothing was going to undo what had happened.

When I realized I was angry about not finding snow boots in my size shortly after finding out an old friend had committed suicide, I realized I was acting as if nothing tough had happened. I knew if I acted like nothing tough had happened, I was never going to make peace with that tough thing. I was always going to be reaching for something to make it go away. And sure, maybe yesterday morning it was only snow boots. But when the snow boots didn't make the pain go away, it would be only a matter of time before I reached for something else, and eventually old patterns and behaviors would find their way back into my life as I settled for easing the pain instead of asking for help. I was looking for snow boots in a size eight, but in that moment I knew buying them would actually be baby steps in a direction I didn't want to go.

I texted my best friend, Anna. Everyone needs an Anna. After saying how sorry she was, Anna asked what was going on inside me. Anna has a gift for asking perfect questions. The way she words questions makes me stop and think, *I don't know. Let me think about that.* Anna is quick to listen, slow to respond; and she allows you the necessary time to feel what you are feeling without trying to fix you. Anna isn't afraid of feeling uncomfortable; she will sit in the awkwardness and let you cry as long as you need to.

I told her I was confused and sad and angry, and trying not to medicate. She asked whether she could call me. I knew she was at work, and I already struggle enough with feeling like a burden (an insecurity I'm working on), so I told her she didn't have to. As I set about to process everything on my own, I signed out of Amazon and decided it was the perfect time to do what I had avoided over the last two months. I looked at my ex-boyfriend's Facebook page. Since I am a masochist or an extremist, I guess I figured that if I was going to feel pain anyways, I might as well feel it in all forms. Just before feeling like I was going to throw up, I texted Anna back. "Okay, yes, please call. I just looked at the ex's Facebook page." In less than one minute. my phone rang.

The truth is, even as a Christian, I don't know how to handle death—more specifically, suicide. I don't know how to address it, how to feel about it, how to process it. I just know it hurts to a degree that can't be explained. Suicide—it's a word there are no other words for. I can barely type it without crying and shaking. But instead of trying to figure out how to address suicide, feel its impact, or process it, I just make someone else's suicide all about me and my inability to cope. It's much easier for me to talk about God being near the brokenhearted when I feel what I feel after seeing my ex-boyfriend's Facebook page. It's not as easy for me to ask God where He was when He saw my friend in those last moments before she took her life.

Perhaps that is my struggle with suicide. It's a struggle with God, with who He is and why He allows what He does. And instead of asking the tough questions, be it because I am afraid of the answer or afraid there will be no answer, I distract myself with snow boots and pictures of my ex.

Anna told me I wasn't alone, that she herself had pulled the whole "looking at the ex's Facebook page" thing as a form of digging the knife in deeper when going through something tough. "I don't think you are alone in how you are prone to handling this, JJ," Anna said. "I just think you are more honest about how you are prone to handling it than most people." Perhaps. Anna suggested I write my friend a letter to tell her how I felt about her suicide. "Tell her you're angry," Anna said.

Anna was right. I was angry, but being angry was what I think I was trying to avoid, because I wasn't just angry at God. I was angry at her, my friend, for what she had done. But I felt wrong for being angry at her since she was gone.

"Just tell her how you feel," Anna said.

And so I did.

I wrote as much as I could before I couldn't handle it anymore. I cried as I packed up my bags to go to the house where I would be staying for Thanksgiving. Then I shut off my tears just as quickly as I shut my laptop.

On the way to my home for the next few days, I spotted a shopping center; and just as quickly as I realized my need to feel the pain when I had been on the phone with Anna, I forgot it upon seeing the shopping center. There were at least four shoe stores, and I went in each one, determined to find some snow boots. While I realized buying something I didn't need wasn't going to fix the pain, the guilt I would feel by spending money I didn't have on something I didn't need would certainly distract me from the pain I felt. If ever there was a self-sabotager, it was I.

I shuffled in store after store. I'm quite certain I looked crazy, especially since I didn't actually want to be in there. I felt gross in the florescent-lit department stores when there was natural sunlight outside, and I'm pretty certain "I feel gross" was plastered across my face. I'm not saying department stores are bad places, and I'm not coming down on those who go to them. I'm just saying that for me personally, department stores or shopping centers of any sort are not where I feel alive, so going there when I'm already struggling with life makes me feel gross, to say the least.

In my letter I told my friend I would grieve her, and I thought that meant I couldn't enjoy the sunshine; nor did I think it was right to enjoy anything that day. And so I held myself hostage in department stores, associating grief with feeling gross because I didn't like my surroundings. With no boots picked out, I walked back to my van. I put the key in and tried to crank it up, but nothing happened. There was no noise, not even a click. It was completely dead. I sat for a second and took a deep breath before asking the Holy Spirit to make my van start. I figured it was worth a shot to at least ask, but nothing happened. I called AAA while thanking God that I had AAA. They told me they would arrive in thirty minutes. I tried not to let panic set in as I wondered what was wrong with my van and how much it would cost to fix it.

I looked at my skateboard sitting on the floor of my van. I had been avoiding it for the last month, perhaps because of its own set of memories. *You can skate around the parking lot,* I heard God or my conscience or some inner voice say to me.

"No," I said back. "I could just go buy some shoes since I have to wait."

The sun is shining, the air is cool, the road is smooth, and you have shoes. You would enjoy skating around the parking lot, I heard in response.

"I don't feel like enjoying anything. No, no, no," I pouted.

I sat in my Volkswagen van, death-gripped to the steering wheel, honestly feeling like God was asking me to simply skateboard around the parking lot. Sometimes God asks big things of us, and sometimes He asks us to simply enjoy the life He has given us.

"I can't. No," I said, feeling like I wasn't allowed to enjoy anything since I was grieving.

"Are you actually grieving by looking for shoes to buy?" God asked. I sat quietly, unable to shake the fact that I felt like God was asking me to skateboard.

I debated back and forth before finally saying, "Okay, fine!" while putting on my worn- out shoes and grabbing my skateboard.

It was the perfect day and the perfect place to skateboard. God was right; the sun was shining, the air was cool, and the road was smooth. I had shoes, and I felt alive as I enjoyed skating around the parking lot.

"Wow," I said to myself, "I forgot how much I enjoy this." As I skated, I started to cry, both because I was grateful I wasn't stuck in a department store and because I was sad. I started to realize grief could involve enjoyment, and in fact enjoying my life allowed me to grieve more because of the depth of pain over a life lost. If life wasn't enjoyable, then not much would be lost when someone died.

Life, though hard, is so, so good; and I realized it was hard for me to stomach the thought of a young girl missing out on the goodness of life because she ended it based on a lie that there was no other way out of the tough stuff. Enjoying my life wasn't taking away from grieving my friend; it was making it more real and rawer as I associated grief with feeling sad over loss instead of associating grief with feeling gross due to my surroundings.

I thanked God for the nudge, and I skated back to my van as I saw AAA show up. An older gentleman named Steve took a look at my battery, which had a broken clamp preventing it from starting. "Just get a new clamp at Pep Boys," Steve said. I was trying to mentally document his advice, and I don't know whether it was the look on my face or the dried tears in my eyes, but Steve paused and with deep sincerity in his voice said, "Why don't you follow me to Pep Boys, and I'll show you what to get."

I thanked him and hopped in my van as we got it running long enough to get to Pep Boys. I followed Steve into the store, trying to hold back tears as I thanked God someone had been there to help me and show me what to do. Steve picked through the brake clamps and handed me on. "Get this one, and I'll put it on for ya." I walked to the cashier, again thanking God I wasn't alone.

Steve pulled out a pink leopard print toolbox from his truck and began working on my battery. "I like that toolbox," I said with a slight laugh.

"Oh yeah," Steve said, "there's a story to that one."

"I wondered," I said. "I figured there'd have to be."

He told me he'd needed a metal toolbox a year and a half ago, and that was the only design they had. "It was forty dollars!" Steve said. "And I wasn't going to pay forty dollars for a toolbox I didn't like, so I figured I'd wait till next season when they got in new ones. I went back a year later, and they didn't have new ones, but they had these on sale for nineteen dollars, so I got two."

I laughed because it sounded all too familiar. In my efforts to save money, I wait for the right time (sale time) instead of buying something I don't like. Then as soon as it goes on sale, I suddenly like it and end up spending the same amount of money I was trying to save. I have ended up with more than one something I originally didn't even like, on more than one occasion.

I heard Steve's dispatcher over the radio ask where he was, and he said he was helping me put a battery clamp on. "We don't normally do that," the dispatcher said. "Let me know when you finish up."

"I know," Steve said. "I'll just be about five more minutes." When Steve was done, he handed me the broken clamp. "Do you wanna keep that?" he asked.

"Yeah," I said, "I'll keep it for the story. I'm a story person."

Steve laughed. "Yeah, there you go. I could tell." I shook his hand and thanked him again. I thanked God for Steve, who'd treated me like a person, not just a customer. And though he didn't know it, he brought some relief and a smile to an aching heart.

I noticed Jiffy Lube across the street, and seeing as how I was well overdue for an oil change, I figured I might as well since I was out, and it was there. I pulled in and was escorted to the outdoor computer, where they plug in all your information. After one guy couldn't get my van to start, the other guys made fun of him for not being able to drive a manual. They pulled my van in, and I explained that the back was a bit tricky to open. "There's a trick, but I don't actually know what it is," I said as I laughed.

"You mean, there's a trick to opening the back of your car, and you don't know it?" a guy named Casey asked sarcastically.

I laughed. "Yeah, it's kind of broken, and so you have to turn and push and pull until something works."

Casey turned and pushed and pulled before a couple of other guys started to gather around to offer help but mostly laugh. "What the what?" Casey laughed. "Is this a trick?"

Five different guys tried to get the back open, and I stood back and laughed harder than I have laughed in a while. "Are you a secret shopper?" Casey asked as all the other guys laughed at him and took turns. I laughed so hard while watching them that my stomach hurt. Then I thanked God that I had gotten to laugh that hard.

"Here, let me try," I said.

There I was at Jiffy Lube, surrounded by five grown men, who unsuccessfully tried to get the back of my van open. When I jumped in to help we finally got it open, in which the glory of my house was revealed.

"There's a bed in there," Casey said. "This is the craziest oil change ever!" They helped me move my bed back since it sat on top of the engine, and when they lifted the bed, Casey took note of the pillows I had stuffed underneath it to keep the bed even.

"What!? Pillows!" he yelled. "She's a pillow smuggler!?"

I laughed so hard I keeled over and almost started to cry simply because it felt so good to laugh that hard. Casey called me "the pillow smuggler" the rest of the time. He had questions about Oregon and about living in a van. The guys helped put my bed back when they were finished.

"I bet you don't normally have a bunch of guys help you make your bed," Casey said. He was right. He helped me with the paperwork and apologized if it was the most awkward oil change ever. "We don't normally touch pretty blankets and pillows with our dirty hands." That made sense, seeing as how most people don't live in their cars or sleep on top of their engines.

I pulled out of Jiffy Lube, feeling a little lighter. Much like Steve, the guys at Jiffy Lube were "just" doing their job, but they'd brought great relief and a lot of laughter to a girl with an aching heart. Little did they know they'd helped mend more than my van. That is why I don't believe in "just" doing anything or ministry being something that happens only in church. The guys at Jiffy Lube didn't know the weight of what I was carrying that day, but they ministered to my heart with laughter and kindness.

I arrived at the house where I would be staying for the next week and let myself in. With no one home, I unloaded my things and grabbed my skateboard to skate around the area as the sun was going down. Earlier that day, the parking lot had given me a taste of what I had been missing, so I set out to clear my head and take in the sunset instead of staying stuck inside, which unfortunately tends to be my default. I thanked God for that day, and I thanked Him that my van had broken down. I thanked Him for the push I'd needed to get out into the light and taste life with all it had to offer, the good and the hard. I thanked God for Steve and the guys at Jiffy Lube. I thanked Him that pain couldn't be cured with something like snow boots. As I skated downhill, I thanked God and took in the cool of the evening, enjoying the sunset. As I walked back uphill, I thought of my friend, and I cried. I cried hard for her and her family.

Back and forth I went, going downhill while thanking God and enjoying the ride and going uphill while crying and feeling the pain, still thanking God for His goodness and the ability to feel. I lay down in the grass and looked up at the stars. I ripped the grass up and held a blade up to my nose. It smelled like grass, which smelled like life. The smell of the grass did something for me the department store couldn't—it made me feel alive, which forced me to thank God for life, which forced me to ask the tough question why. Why did she give up on life? But more so, why did He allow it? It took four department stores to get me to avoid the question and only one blade of grass to ask it (the works of man have got nothing on the works of God).

Why?

I still don't have the answers. Maybe I never will. Maybe some things in life we won't understand on this side of eternity, and I'll be the first to say it's not fair. I don't know. But I do know that living as if it's not fair is no way to live, and not living is no way to honor, or at the very least grieve, those you've lost.

When things like this happen, I don't understand Jesus. I still love Him; I just don't understand Him. But instead of not dealing with the issue by trying to figure Him out and staying angry at Him until I do, I'm going to do what He did when He lost someone He loved. Jesus wept.

While this might not be the best way to come to a close, I do so knowing there will be a time to dance (since there is a season for everything). But for now I weep, just as my Savior did, and I grieve. And though external circumstances or feelings tempt me to believe otherwise, I choose to believe and claim God is good, even when it doesn't feel like it. And I will look for His goodness in the simplest of places, be it in a broken battery, an awkward oil change, or a single blade of grass that smells like life.

My Mommom

We don't have a Christmas tree this year. I suppose at thirty-two years old and with all that is going on in the world, it isn't the biggest deal that we don't have a Christmas tree this year. In the grand scheme of things, it isn't a big deal at all. Plenty of people either don't have Christmas trees or have never had one, so who am I to complain?

And yet I've been thinking (shocker). If I can so easily dismiss my feelings about not having a Christmas tree this year, I can just as easily dismiss someone else's feelings about not having a Christmas tree this year, which is to say I can easily dismiss their story without a care in the world as to the reason why they didn't have a Christmas tree this year or maybe why they never had one at all (if they, in fact, celebrate Christmas).

Perhaps it's not so much about the Christmas tree as it is about the *why* behind it. As with many things in life that may seem like no big deal, perhaps the small things are a big deal because there is a *why* attached to those small things, a story unheard due to assumptions.

I've always been obsessed with Christmas. I was the kid who was preparing for the arrival of December 25th the day after Halloween and honestly sometimes even before then. My goal was to turn our house into a winter wonderland no matter how tacky everyone else thought it to be. I hung lights anywhere my mother would allow them and spent any extra money I had on decorations.

As a preacher's kid, I understood "the reason for the season," but as just your average kid, the manger scene was more of an epic centerpiece for Christmas dinner. I was grateful Jesus had come to earth in the form of a little baby, mostly because it gave us a reason to have Christmas—the ultimate birthday party.

When I was really young, my gifts consisted of coupon books, ones that included free hugs, a three-minute back rub, being nice to my sister, Betsy ... stuff like that. When I got older, the coupons became more serious: extended free hugs, ten-minute back rubs, and kisses for the whole family, even when I didn't feel like kissing them. My mom still has the coupons.

In college my gift to my parents was my presence at home, because like your average college kid, I was broke. But with my presence came my Christmas spirit and ability to decorate. I'd stay up late on Christmas Eve (after the roles reversed and the parents were the first to go to bed) to clean the entire house, set and decorate the kitchen table for the Christmas meals, and prepare an overnight breakfast casserole to be served alongside Jesus's birthday cake in the morning.

When I started working, the presents came rolling in, and without the excuse of being a kid, I lost complete sense of what Christmas was all about. I tried to make the day last as long as possible by getting as many presents as possible. The longer we all sat around the tree and opened presents, the better Christmas seemed. Maybe somewhere deep down, it wasn't so much about the presents; maybe it was just wanting my family to sit around together for an extended period in which they all seemed happy; and maybe without the presents, I didn't know how else to make that happen.

The Christmas of 2006 was the worst Christmas I can remember, largely due to my eating disorder and the inability to fix it with the Christmas spirit. I racked up a great deal of debt that season because shopping kept me from binging and purging on the Christmas cookies I made in abundance (because one batch of cookies is never enough for a bulimic). My old friend anorexia would sometimes come to visit, and on those days I felt powerful and in control, but my newer friend bulimia liked the holidays more than anorexia, and so bulimia was who I spent more of my time with that holiday season. I tried so hard to make Christmas perfect that year, and all I can remember is how miserable I was.

After going off to treatment in 2007, it would be a couple of years before I returned home again for Christmas. In 2009, when I finally did go home, I was unaware that it was going to be the last Christmas when my whole family would be together, my parents still living under the same roof. I was sick and slept through Christmas dinner. My boyfriend at the time had flown in from Chicago to surprise me, but seeing as how I had passed out on the couch, he ended up spending most of his time talking to my grandmother, an often-forgotten family member.

After moving to Portland, Oregon, in the fall of 2010, I spent the following Christmases out on the West Coast with friends. Friends are often easier than family and much cheaper than a round-trip ticket across the United States, so my excuses to stay away from home were valid.

Last year I returned home for Christmas, and it was the first time members of my family celebrated in two different houses due to my parents' divorce. I didn't know how to feel about it. I tried to make the best of it, as I was advised to do, but what about the reality of it being sad that we weren't one family anymore? I mean, sure, we were, but we weren't.

I didn't think I would be back home for Christmas this year. It wasn't part of my plan; funny how that works. I'd been living in San Diego, California, over the past year, and San Diego was perfect for escaping life's problems, except for the fact that you never escape life's problems no matter where you go. After going on a trip overseas with my mom and brother, I returned to South Carolina with them. That was in October, and I'm still here … at Christmas.

I've spent the last few months helping my mother move out of our family home of thirty-five years. The house is on the market, and if ever there were an empty nest, it is that house. Day in and day out, my mother, brother, and I have stripped the walls and packed everything away, taking car load after car load over to my mother's new condo. It's been a slow process, and I'm exhausted. *Make the best of it,* I hear a voice say in the back of my mind, and so I've been trying to do that—make the best of it, offer help, cook food, be present, be strong, be thirty-two and not in need of a Christmas tree.

A couple of weeks ago, I was in the empty house by myself. I turned on Christmas music and let it echo through the empty halls. I danced, and I was happy. Then I sat on the floor of the larger-than-life, empty living room and watched memories flash across the walls as if they were movie clips, and I cried. For the first time since my family had split up, I uttered the words "I miss my family." I lay on the floor and cried as I let myself miss my family. "I wish we had a Christmas tree," I cried, but I knew it was about more than just the tree.

It's no secret that I'm an advocate of feeling your pain, in part because I've spent a good portion of my life avoiding it. But as of recently, I'm sick of feeling my pain to the point of not being able to see other people. I'm still trying to find the balance of feeling your feelings without getting stuck in them. And so while I'm bummed we don't have a Christmas tree because my mom's condo is too small, our old house is too empty, and I'm still not quite sure who to spend Christmas with or how, this doesn't have to be the Christmas that gets remembered as the one without the tree.

In the middle of all the moving and family drama and stress of holiday expectations, there is someone I overlooked along the way, someone I've overlooked along the entire way, as in the span of my entire life.

My mother's mother. Mommom, we call her. My grandmother, Betty.

My grandmother still remembers that boy who talked to her at Christmas dinner in 2009. She asked about him the other day, and when I told her we had been broken up for five years and that he had been dating someone else for the last three, she responded with "Aww, shame. I always liked him." I found her response to be funny, seeing as how she'd met him only once, but at the same time I knew why she felt this way. She felt this way because even if it had been just for a short while on a night five years ago, she'd felt seen and noticed and paid attention to. No one forgets that feeling.

I have spent the last couple of months getting to know this forgotten member of my family, my grandmother. She was always present at holidays, providing shrimp on Christmas Eve, gifting us with at least two dollars for each kid so we could "treat ourselves," and snoring on the couch in the late afternoons. I have memories of her in the background, and for the most part, that is all— background memories.

One morning I was trying to figure out how I could do more to help other people, to step outside of my own selfish head and meet the needs of others. I knew I was limited as to what I could do financially, but relationally I had something to offer, which is sometimes the harder thing to give. Handing someone money or a piece of pie is often easier than sitting down next to them and trying to figure out what to talk about, especially in this day and age when everyone has to be so politically correct that people are afraid to talk anymore. Not to mention the distraction of cell phones, which has left this generation of teenagers crippled from being able to make eye contact.

And let's be honest; it's not just the teenagers. I see kids playing at the park while their parents scroll through their Instagram or check their e-mail on a park bench. I myself will sit next to my grandmother with my head buried in my phone, clicking likes on pictures of people helping people while I'm ignoring the lonely woman beside me.

And such was the case that morning when I was admiring others on social media for doing so much for others while I sat on a couch next to my grandmother, who was staring at the wall. I immediately started to look up ways I could volunteer, especially over the holidays. It didn't cross my mind that sitting beside me was a woman in need of love and attention and eye contact just as much as people in the nursing home or on the street. The ugly truth is, it didn't feel as good to help or even love my grandmother as it did to help or love other people I had no history with, who would praise me for my efforts.

After spending the day looking up good causes, journaling, praying, and trying to "get right with God," I decided I would go for a run at sunset. It seemed to be just what I needed. As I passed through the kitchen to grab some water before heading out, I noticed my grandmother trying to cut an onion. I asked her what she was doing, and she said she was trying to make dinner. My mom wouldn't be getting off work until around dinner time, and Mommom sometimes tries to cook on designated nights to help out.

Assuming Mommom wanted to feel like she was contributing, I let her carry on. I so often function out of assumption; I think we all do, but I'll speak for myself. I'm embarrassed to say it, but multiple times I have walked past my grandmother trying to chop an onion in the kitchen, while thinking, *Good job, Mommom,* instead of, *Hey, can I help?* And I get it; not everybody wants help. Some people want to chop their own onions and show the world or at least their grandchildren they are capable of chopping their own onions, which is great. Chop away! But I think asking whether help is needed, which is just initiating a conversation if nothing else, is worth the risk of your offer being rejected.

I grabbed my headphones and running shoes, and I walked back through the kitchen. I sat at the table and looked at Mommom. She was barely five feet tall, her white bushy hair giving her an extra inch, while hunched over the kitchen counter trying to chop an onion. I watched her as I put my shoes on. She moved slower than I remembered. I lingered for a second, which is sometimes all the time needed to grab one's attention.

I wanted to offer her help because I knew it was the right thing to do, but truth be told, in getting back to the basics of calling a spade a spade, I didn't want to offer help because it got in the way of my plans.

I didn't want to offer help *to my own grandmother.* And even if we weren't related, she was an elderly human being. And even if she weren't elderly, she was a human being. In that moment of hesitating to offer her help, the content of my character was revealed, and I realized I didn't actually want to step outside of myself and help people. I wanted to *feel good* about helping people so long as they didn't interfere with my plans. I still wanted life to be all about me. No matter how many times I learn the lesson, my wayward heart sets itself on myself, and I forget that people matter.

Sometimes I forget that I matter, and I wear myself out in an attempt to do everything for other people. And once I've burned myself out, I jump to the other extreme, forgetting that other people matter, writing them off in an attempt to take care of only myself. I struggle to find the balance between the two. The simple balance of *all* people mattering—other people and me.

I watched my grandmother struggle to chop an onion. I stood up, picked up my iPod, took a deep breath, and set it back down. "Do you need any help, Mommom?" I asked, honestly kind of hoping she would say no so I could still go for a run *and* feel good about offering help.

She didn't respond. Between my hesitant attempt to gently offer help and Mommom's hearing aids not always working, I realized she didn't hear me.

"MOMMOM," I yelled, *"DO YOU NEED ANY HELP?"*

Mommom turned around to look at me. "Did you say something?" she asked.

I laughed a little to myself. *"YES!"* I yelled. *"I asked if you needed any help!"*

Mommom's face lit up, "Ohhhhhhhh!" she said excitedly. "Wow-wee, that would be wonderful. I can't move as fast as I used to. We might never eat at the rate I'm moving."

I laughed but also felt a few degrees more horrible for not asking before then whether she needed help. I knew I wasn't going to get my run in that day, but I also knew something else mattered more, even if (for as much as I hate to admit it) helping with dinner didn't feel like it mattered more in the moment. I am selfish through and through, to the point of it blinding me to help the older woman, who was struggling right before my eyes.

For some reason it's easy to dismiss helping the older woman when she is my grandmother, assuming she will always be there and she can hold her own. But there will come a time when she won't always be there, and she can't hold her own anymore. In which case I have to ask myself, "Am I going to run away because it feels better, or am I going to step into someone else's struggle ... just because?"

I began to cut the onions, mash the potatoes, and set the table, all the while making jokes with Mommom and repeating them louder so she could hear me. As I helped with dinner that night, I knew a friendship was being formed, and there was the realization that even when I think I have nothing to give, I always have a helping hand to offer and a really loud joke to tell that can bring a smile to a weary soul.

At thirty-two years old, my friendship with my grandmother began. We've clearly always been related, but we've never actually been friends. In part this is because I had the shocking revelation that I'd never actually sat down with my grandmother and said. "Tell me about you." I began to ask my grandmother questions, first over time spent making dinner, then over time spent having tea in the late afternoons. Mommom would talk about her own mother with a smile, and it was clear she loved her mother very much. It was the first time I saw my grandmother as someone's daughter and not just a distant relative.

As I began to see my grandmother as someone's daughter, I realized I could relate to her because I was someone's daughter. The more I listened to Mommom's stories, the more affection I felt for her. I began looking for ways to help her, going out of my way to ensure her comfort, not just because she was an old lady but because she was my friend.

I didn't hear Mommom say, "I love you" very much while I was growing up, which isn't to say she didn't love us. Some people just never learn how to express love, or they learn and then somewhere along the way of life throwing a few heavy hits, they forget. The few times I remember saying, "I love you" to Mommom were only slightly less awkward than her reaction of, "Okay, you too." Some people don't know how to receive love either, and after you hear their story, it makes sense as to why.

As my affection has grown for my grandmother over the last three months, so has my ability to communicate my love for her. *"I LOVE YOU MOMMOM!"* I'd yell (so she could hear me) before leaving the house. In the beginning she'd respond with her awkward, quiet whisper, "Okay, you too." Over time she progressed to awkwardly whisper, "Love you too," as if she were unsure she could say it or not. Regardless of whether I got the response I wanted, I continued to tell her I loved her because I did, and it mattered less and less what the response was. I'd rub lotion on her legs, drive her to the doctor, carry her meal tray to the table, put a sweet treat on her plate, and look for little ways not just to say, "I love you" but to show her I did.

Over time those little things have added up, and Mommom, growing more and more into knowing she is loved and cared for, has begun to liven up in a way I didn't see while I was growing up; in part because I didn't really see her and in another part because some of her difficult experiences in life added up to her being unsure of how to give and receive love. Now, before I leave the house, Mommom yells with confidence, *"I SURE DO LOVE YOU, JJ!"*

I kiss her on the cheek, look her in the eyes, and say, "I love *you*, Mommom."

Love is hard, and I don't mean that in a cliché way, although maybe it's cliché for a reason—because it's true. When you really stop (really stop) and think about living out the task of loving someone, no matter what the cost is to you or whether you get it back, and you do it day in and day out all the days of your life … love is hard. We all know by now that love isn't a feeling, and I know people need things to be defined so they call love a choice (since it's not a feeling), and yes, it is a choice, choosing to act out love even when you don't feel it, but I think love is even more than a choice. I think love is so much grander than we could ever imagine or hope to express or receive that quite simply there isn't a category to put it in or another word to define it ... it just is. Love is what it is—it's love. Love surpasses all understanding, all realm of thinking, all reason, all logic, and honestly, it makes no sense.

But for as hard as love is, I honestly believe it's worth it. I believe that love is hard and life is good, and that love is good and life is hard. I believe that it's both for everyone and that it's okay for both to be good and both to be hard.

A few months ago, I set out to travel and be adventurous and meet new people, because to me that was the definition of life being good. Instead, I somehow managed to spend most of that time at home, my very definition of life being hard. But I found out that whether you are traveling or stationary, life is both good and hard, and wherever you go, there you are. While I haven't traveled as much as I'd hoped these last few months, I did make a new friend I didn't see coming—my grandmother, my Mommom. It has been since being at home that I've realized if you try to avoid the hard parts of life, you'll end up missing out on the really, really good parts.

It's not like everything is fixed at home; nor is it a Cinderella story of happily ever after. We still celebrate Christmas in two different houses, but it's a hopeful story of no matter my circumstance or how hard life and love may get, it is well with my soul.

And well worth the journey.

Simple Wonders

A dear friend of mine decided to get married on New Year's Eve in San Diego. After I spent the last three months in South Carolina, her wedding had called me back to the California coast I call home. I packed up my things, flew halfway across the country, landed in Texas, and hopped a ride to drive the rest of the way back to California. I love to travel. I love being in the act of it, anticipating where I am going, being present where I am, finding the balance between the two, and making room for both. Sometimes I take the long way to the grocery store just so I can travel a little bit longer.

Truth be told, I could have passed up going to my friend's wedding for the sake of travel, but deep down something in me knew something about this life had more to do with people than it did with how many locations I could get to in one road trip, and so unlike myself, I hurried home.

I made it just in time to see my friend walk down the aisle. She was every color of beautiful, in part because the colorful tattoos all over her body made the white in her dress shine an extra shade of bright, and in part because I could tell her heart was about to explode with joy as she held her breath to walk toward the man she wanted to spend the rest of her life with. She made her way down the aisle, caught a glimpse of me in the audience, and as if to be further surprised by joy, she mouthed, "Oh, JJ!" She held back tears and smiled. My heart leaped, and everything about rushing home was 110 percent worth it.

"Relationships," I whispered to myself, "people. There's something about people that I know this life is about. Even when it doesn't seem like it matters, it does."

We danced the night away at her wedding. She shares the same affection I do for nineties hip-hop culture, so between Mariah Carey and Boyz II Men, we could have broken the concrete floor with how hard we danced. "Dancing," I whispered to myself. "There is something eternal about it. I feel too alive when I do it for it not to last forever."

We sent my friend and her husband off in style, with sparklers and chants and fist pumps to the air or to God, whichever your preference.

The wedding reception ended with a long night still ahead of us. In eager anticipation of welcoming in a new year, my friend and I wanted to keep dancing, but seeing as how we aren't as young as we used to be, we get tired earlier in the evening. I'll speak for myself. Knowing we didn't feel up to bar hopping but didn't want to go back home, we drove out to Shelter Island to get the perfect view of the city. The moon hung low over downtown San Diego, nearly touching the tops of the tall buildings.

We made plans to come back out one night and take pictures, a plan still sitting patiently on our to-do list. After driving up and down the little island, we noticed a hotel still lit up for Christmas with welcoming doors. People were walking in and out, some on smoke breaks, some on cell phones. Figuring it must be some kind of New Year's Eve party, we decided to venture over.

There was an older man sitting out front who noticed us looking in the windows. "Just walk in like you own the place, turn to the right, go all the way back, and there is a live band with dancing." Perhaps it was obvious we wanted to be involved with what was going on but didn't actually know what was going on.

"Oh! Thank you!" we said, and with that I adjusted my jacket to make it look like I owned the place, opened the door, and walked in.

We followed the sound of a live band to a room full of dancing. My friend and I appeared to be thirty years younger than everyone but maintained an "I own this place" attitude while still smiling and trying to appear kind. I watched while the band played Stevie Wonder songs and older-to-elderly people got down on the dance floor. *This is gold,* I thought. "We're totally staying here," I said to my friend.

"Oh, absolutely we are," she said, and our friendship made sense.

We danced until the ball dropped with perfect strangers imperfectly dancing. We welcomed in the new year with people thirty years our senior, and even though we didn't know each other, something about the whole thing felt eternal; all of us were celebrating together for one cause as if we were family. Perhaps it was the dancing, perhaps it was the coming together of different generations, and perhaps it was Stevie Wonder.

It was the best New Year's I can remember having in a long time. Maybe at some point we all say that. Maybe there's a point in which some people never say that. I tend to forget that New Year's isn't just some holiday in which I deserve to have a good time. Having fun on New Year's Eve isn't a right; for some people it's just another night of trying to figure out how they are going to make it through. In those moments of realization, I feel helpless, crippled by anxiety over the state of humanity, which is the exact type of thought you're told to put away on occasions like New Year's. After all, you don't want to be Debbie Downer at the party. I don't know where the balance is between living your life and keeping aware of the lives of others, but I think it might be somewhere in between gratitude and time and action.

I'm grateful I had such a good New Year's, because not everyone gets one, I'm even grateful I allowed myself to have such a good New Year's. Had I sat on my worries about the state of the world, I would have missed out on the people right in front of me—not only my friend, whom I had the time of my life with, but also the people whose story I don't know, who may have had a hard year despite what their expensive dress said.

Now that I am back in San Diego with a new year ahead of me, I am excited about what is to come; I'm nervous too but mostly excited. I set out to go for a walk the other day, and less than a minute into my walk, I ran into Richard, my seventy-plus-year-old neighbor. He asked over and over again how I had been and where I had been and said he was worried about me. Three months are a long time, and I didn't get to see him before I left. "I thought something had happened to ya," he said. "I went down to your coffee shop and asked about ya." Richard and I visited with each other often. The first time I met him, he helped me put air in my bike tires. The second time we went for a bike ride all over the city.

Richard told me about how worried he had been. "I thought something happened to ya," he said over and over again. "I didn't know you were leaving ... Are you glad to be back? It's good to be back, right?" he asked, almost nervous I might leave again. I felt both happy that Richard was so anxious to see me and sad that I hadn't told him I was leaving. Honestly, I didn't think it mattered, only because I had forgotten that when it comes to people, even when it doesn't seem like it matters, it does. I didn't realize what our frequent run-ins had meant to him. I felt happy that Richard would care so much about me and sad that I would be so careless with him. *I want to be more intentional with people,* I thought.

Richard invited me in to share some ideas with me. As he asked what my plans for myself were, he said he had an idea. "Can you play a guitar?" he asked.

I said I could.

"Can you carry a tune?" he asked.

I said I could ... well enough.

"You start practicing every day, get yourself twenty-five minutes' worth of material. You think you could do that ... be in front of people for twenty-five minutes?"

I laughed, thinking about where he was going with his idea. "Yeah, between stories and jokes and singing, I think I could last twenty-five minutes."

"Good," he said with excitement. "Now you get yourself an act, practice every day, record a little demo, and send it to people. You start driving up the coast in your van and send the demo to people to say you're coming. Then you can perform in places all the way up to Oregon."

He laughed and smiled as he carried on planning my "career" as a performer. "Not everyone can do it," he says, "but you could. You got the personality. You could do it!"

I noticed a guitar in the corner of Richard's living room. "Do you play?" I asked.

He said he did as he laughed and waved his hand. "Not so much anymore, but I used to."

I asked whether he could teach me a thing or two on the guitar.

"You don't need a teacher," he said, "if you got the basic skills, which you do, right?" I nodded. "Then all you have to do is practice every day. So many people want to move on to the next thing and do all this fancy stuff, but they never master the basics, so they never really learn to get better. They just find new tricks."

I thought this to be true to my life in many ways. I was always anxious to move on to the next bigger and better thing without really taking the time to invest in understanding the basics, like loving people well, sending them thank-you cards, and letting them know I was leaving town and wouldn't be back for a really long time (not to worry).

I asked Richard whether he would play his guitar for me one night, and he agreed that he would. He went back to talking about my plan to drive up the coast and perform in music venues and coffee houses. "And listen up," he said. "You get paid to do this ... no freebies! People are gonna want you to perform for free, but you say no. I mean, every now and then a freebie is okay. It's good to give back, but you can't do all freebies. You gotta get paid." He smiled and stared off into the distance as if he were reliving a dream. "Yeah, you could just drive up the coast and play at night. It would be wonderful." I agreed that it would. "I'd do it myself," he said, "but I'm too old." He laughed at the thought. "Think about it," he said before I left. "You could take your van, plus you'd be good at it. You'd make people laugh."

I thanked Richard and gave him a hug before I left. We planned our next bike ride. I walked to the coffee shop where I used to work and was greeted with hugs and screams of excitement. "Yeaaah!" my friend yelled. "I'm just so excited. I want to pick you up and pace back and forth with you in my arms!" So she did. My heart felt happy and loved. I walked to the bank to pray there'd be money in my account, also to deposit a small check, which was an answer to prayer (a combination of human initiative and divine interaction). I thanked God.

I walked down Newport Avenue, the main street in town, and I took in those fresh feelings of returning home. I took note of everyone I walked past, seeing some familiar faces hidden in the herds of tourists. I high-fived a friend coming out of his shop. I felt like I was right where I belonged. I walked to the end of the street that dead-ended at the ocean. Everything had its place: the seagulls, the buskers singing at the ocean's edge, the surfers gliding across the water, even the tourists walking aimlessly around, taking pictures. Everything seemed to be just as I had left it, and everyone seemed to belong, even the tourists.

I took in a deep breath to smell the salt water. I thanked God I was alive and that I lived in Ocean Beach, California.

Last year was tough despite what social media suggests, but I'm sure that could be true for many if not most people. I was nervous to come back to California. I was nervous to have a repeat of last year, and seeing as how that was the last thing I wanted, I almost resorted to not coming back. While it's always an option to leave when the going gets tough, it's also a way to miss out on the goodness of life, some of which is so simple you could easily miss it.

Rejoicing at my friend's wedding, sitting in Richard's living room, hugging my coworkers, high-fiving my friend on the street, and smelling the ocean air are all simple joys I would have missed had I not come back to California, not to mention prolonging panic mode as I tried to figure out what to do next. I so easily forget that my past experience doesn't have to define my present one, and that while I might have made mistakes before, it doesn't mean I'm destined to repeat them. Prone to, yes. As humans we are all prone to repeating our mistakes. Half the battle is being aware of that, but destined to? Absolutely not.

And so for now, I'm at peace with the home of my childhood and pleased to be back in the place that has become my home later in life. I'm not traveling as much, but I'm enjoying my neighbors and living the adventure of doing everyday life with the people around me. It is an odd combination of simple and wonderful, but I think that is what the best stories are made up of ... the simple wonders that take place when you love the people in front of you.

Goodbye for Now

Epilogue

Over four years have gone by since my book was funded to be published. Shortly after writing "A Single Blade of Grass," I stopped writing for a while. The problem with not writing was the timing. I had just received funding for the publication of this book by a group effort made by people from all over. It wasn't the best time to stop writing. As 2015 approached, my job at the church I worked for came to an end. I reconnected and disconnected with my ex once more (old habits die hard). I eventually moved out of my van into a beach house and started a job at a local coffee shop in Ocean Beach, California ... the one where my coworker fed me bleach. It's been a whirlwind of a year.

Somewhere in that year, I made a few stabs at trying to write again, but mostly it just looked like me sitting down at my desk and two minutes later having a complete meltdown because I was convinced I had lost my ability to write. It was all way too much pressure, and I just simply couldn't do it. I resorted to asking God for help through my tears, and when nothing magical happened, I resorted to peanut butter. I've gained nearly ten pounds since getting my book funded ... exercise included. Crying burns calories, right?

I gave up trying to publish this book until the morning I found myself choking on bleach. While choking, well aware of the fact that I wasn't going to die, even if it was all going to be bad for a while, I knew that living through the incident for the sake of surviving and doing nothing with the life I've been given was just as much, if not more, of a death sentence. "You're going to live through this, JJ," I kept saying to myself, "but once this is all over, it's your choice if you really live or not." While I was grateful that a dose of bleach and a dirty floor were not the elements included in my death, I didn't necessarily want to go back to the life I had recently been living, one of being apathetic and settling and having fun from time to time but not much else.

With a burned throat and a heavy heart due to disappointment in myself for missing it again, I called my best friend, Anna. "As I prayed for you on Wednesday," Anna said, "I kinda got this sense that God is concerned that you take the obligation of writing the book (with the support from all these people) more seriously than the fact that He called you into this, and He wants to challenge, strengthen, delight, know, and relate with you in this. It's not even about the book, though I think that will come through. He called you into this because He loves you ... a lot."

Knowing Anna was right, I remembered that God hadn't placed a burden on me to live up to impossible standards. Publishing this book wasn't something I *had* to do; it was something I *got* to do, because that's how God is. He delights in His children and loves seeing them enjoy themselves, especially when they are doing what they were created to do. To not be able to write as a writer feels like being undead—not dead but not alive either. God wants me to write because I love writing. Sometimes the really big stuff is actually so small and simple.

I wasn't even sure I "should" still publish this—by the time it comes out, years will have passed, relationships will have changed and my heart will certainly have recovered from the weary state it was in when I first set out to write. But, so as to honor myself (even if my former self) and my desire to do what I was created to do (no matter how much time has passed), I will finish what I started. Maybe that alone will encourage others to not give up, to keep moving forward and to believe they are worth pursuing what makes them feel most alive.

I still struggle with calling a spade a spade. While some authors are experts on the subject matter they publish, I still struggle with mine. I fully believe in the truth setting you and me free, and I think when I am most honest, I want the feeling of having told the truth without actually having to tell it. I want the freedom without the process it takes to get there. I used to think risk-taking involved extreme sports, but I think the greater risks in life involve confession and vulnerability.

God hasn't changed some of my circumstances like I wish He would. I cannot claim to understand God or the way He works. I cannot even claim to always agree with God or the way He writes stories. Sometimes I want the pen back. But whether God fixes my broken heart, redeems my family's story, or gives me a better one doesn't matter because it's not the point. The point isn't what God may or may not do for any of us. The point is that He is able to do any and everything, above and beyond all we could think, hope, imagine, or dare to ask for (Ephesians 3:20). And as His children, His own personal creations, we can trust Him with what He may or may not do.

Above all, I truly believe there is a peace offered to everyone that passes all understanding in this world. It is a peace in the midst of chaos and a peace to be felt in the midst of feeling your pain instead of running away from it. It is a peace that doesn't promise warm fuzzies, holy hugs, or flower headbands. It is a peace in knowing that even when all seems lost, you are not forgotten and alone. *You are valuable beyond belief, and you matter incredibly.*

In knowing this about yourself, you don't need to live from a place of self-defense or a need for power, money, or success but from a place of knowing that what is true for you is also true for other people. No matter how different they are, they are not forgotten and alone; they are valuable beyond belief, and they matter incredibly, so treat them accordingly.

And so perhaps that is the last spade I will call as I close this book and continue to live my story. Though I haven't done the best job of living like I believe it, and though I often try too hard to be relevant and liked by a world that doesn't recognize Him, I really do believe Jesus is the answer for the human heart.

Sometimes God feels as close to me as my hair against my face. Other days I wonder where He went and whether He ever cared at all, but it is on those days that, despite how I feel, I choose to believe that without having done anything or impressed anyone, my heavenly Father has already given me the worth I so desperately seek in this world.

My prayer for you is that you will know this to be true for yourself. You are a child who belongs to Someone who cares, and you are so incredibly worth the life you've been given. May that be the truth that sets you free to be loved for who you really are and not for who you think you have to be. May you embrace the totality of this imperfect life: the ups and downs, the goods and bads, the greats and not-so-greats. May you know you are not alone in your struggle, and may you live victoriously with beautiful battle scars.

In the words of my favorite eight-year-old, who has grown into one of my favorite people, "We're all real good and sad. Jesus will help us."

Thank Y'all

I was instructed to write "acknowledgements," but that's a little too formal for me and I wanted more time and space to really say *thank you* to these people. It takes a village, and my village is spread out by distance and time and seasons of life.

Thank you to all the people who supported the funding of this book five years ago (at this point)! Thank you to those who spread the word, sent notes of encouragement, donated financially and prayed for me during this process. Thank you for your patience as I went through it. In more ways than one, I couldn't have done this without you. Thank you, Presapio family, for your amazing effort to make this book possible—I hope the homemade peanut butter was worth the wait.

Thank you, Evan Hunt, for the season we got to work together at church. You are a better leader than you know. Thank you for wanting me to be me, challenging me to be better, and being a friend even when it was hard. Thank you, Kathliene Sundt, for helping me feel a little less crazy at a time when I felt the craziest and for assuring me that if I was crazy, I had good company. You are crazy-good company; if it wasn't for you, I would have jumped ship a long time ago. Thank you, Abby Meyers, for being an epic pen pal and a constant encouragement to my sometimes-weary soul. You were one of the first people to call me a writer, and I will always be glad your son asked me out for coffee.

Thank you, Liz and Ben Michel. I had no idea the night I saw you dressed as jellyfish that one day you'd be the first ones beside my hospital bed the morning after December 15, 2013; or that you'd be the biggest support in my van life adventures. I love y'all. I don't do happily ever afters, but if Edith needs a fairly good godmother, I'd like to nominate myself.

Thank you, Liz Vice, for having countless FaceTime calls, enjoying late-night chats and prayers, and continuously saying to me, "You are going to write a book." Thank you for singing me to sleep on hard nights and for the bottle of change that changed the path I was taking. Everyone should hear you sing and buy your album at LizVice.com. Thank you, Emily Dauber, for being my longest friend through life's many ups and downs. Your ability to call the truth out of dark places has inspired me to strive for an honest life and extending myself grace when it isn't perfect.

Thank you, Sher Sheets, for gingerbread lattes, strips of bacon, and a faithful friendship through changing seasons. You are one of the few (because you're a four) who knows the stories behind the stories, and that is important to me. When I'm with you, I laugh hard, and I learn a lot about the heart of Jesus. You're a special snowflake.

Thank you, Anna Stewart, for being such a good friend, a best friend, even when it hasn't been easy. Thank you for seeing so much of my mess and always still believing in me because you believe in the good of God and what He wants for His children. Thank you for reminding me constantly that He is a good, good Father and that He loves me madly. Thank you, Grace Stewart, for reminding me there is power in the spoken word and for being the first person to make me speak the words "I'm going to write a book." Five years later, it is finished.

Thank you, Jena Willard, for being the best friend I met later in life. From spontaneous adventures to mundane everyday life, you are the friend I prayed for when I first moved to Ocean Beach. You are what made our house a home. You also introduced me to the guy who would become my best friend for the rest of my life! Which is also to say, thank you, Josh Newton, for coming along later in this journey, supporting me along the way and marrying me just as I am as we grow and change together. Chomp!

Thank you, Dad, for loving me just as I am, for going with me when I left home and went to rehab, for being there when I got out. Between my extreme measures of either wanting to hide under the rug or rip the rug out from everybody, I know I haven't been the easiest to do life with, but your consistent love and care for my well-being have gotten me through some tough times; and I'm glad you're my dad. I love you!

Thank you, Bonnie, for teaching me to smoke my first cigarette at a much too young age but being the first to tell me I should quit by the time I hit college. I know we're all trying to figure this life stuff out, and being the oldest of four is no easy feat, but you are a good mix of having fun while being protective and a really good big sister.

Thank you, Bobby, for watching reruns of *Lost* together every night over the last few months. It has been the perfect outlet to step outside of life's messes, take a break from this book, and spend time with someone I've always wanted to be good friends with—my brother. You're my favorite one.

Thank you, Betsy, for being such a big supporter of this book (*in the final countdown!*). I admit I've always been a little jealous of you, but when I put my insecurities aside and just look at you, I see a talented woman with a sense of humor to match, and I am proud to be your big sister. Sorry it took me so long to realize that was my role (middle-child syndrome). You are one of the gifted few who speaks the same love language as me ... movie quotes.

Thank you, my Marmie, for being the example I never knew I needed of what it looks like to be a strong woman. Your courage in these later years of life has inspired me not to give up on myself just because life has thrown some punches. You have a way of turning punches into puns and mourning into dancing, all while knowing when it's time to be still and let out a good cry. You are a beautiful, resilient human being, and I'm proud to be yours. Thank you for gifting me with time away and a place to rest during the last few months of finishing my book. I think this conversation, which I recorded during my time home, best sums up our honest friendship:

JJ: Here's your change from Blockbuster, Mom.

Mom: That's only thirty cents. I gave you six dollars. How much was the movie you rented?

JJ: Ninety-nine cents.

Mom: Ninety-nine cents? So where's the rest of the money?

JJ: And I bought a movie for four dollars, plus tax.

Mom: You *bought* a movie? With the money I gave you to *rent* a movie?

JJ: Yes

Mom: And your conscience is clear?

JJ: Yes

Mom: I think you should switch therapists.

Rest in peace, Blockbuster.

I love you, Mom.